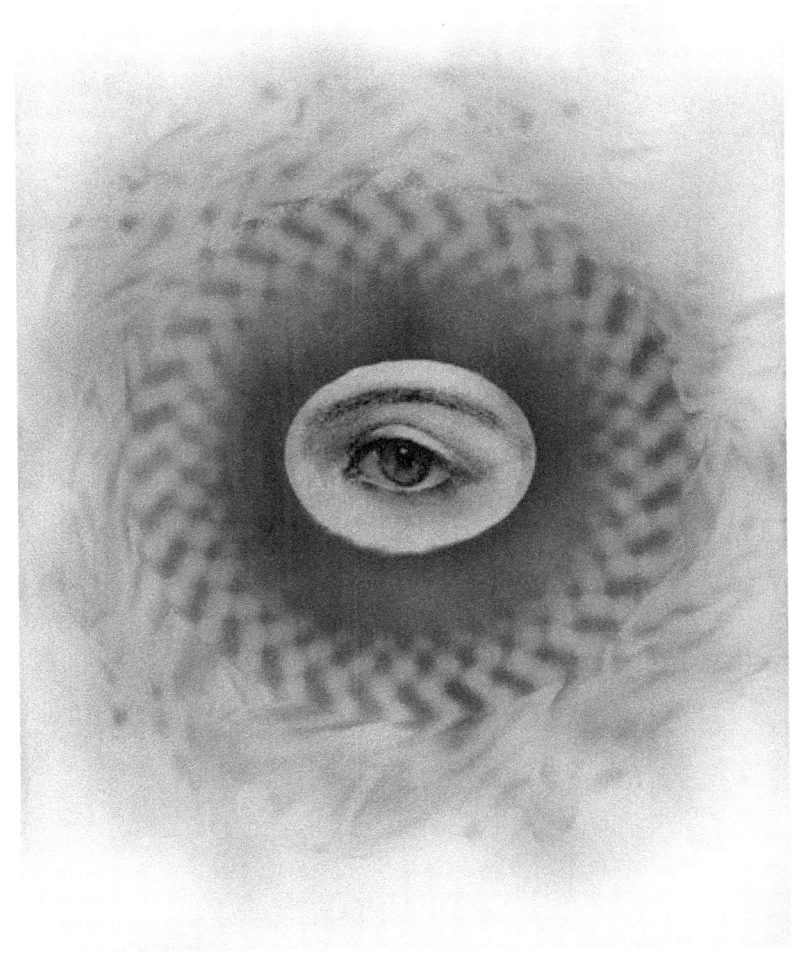

Watching Thought
by
Walter Dutchak (wladicus)
(c) 2013

wd

Watching Thought

By Walter Dutchak
Copyright 2013 Walter Dutchak

* * * *

ISBN: 978-0-9693199-9-3

* * * *

Other Books by this Author

Thoughts and Time

*

wd

TABLE of CONTENTS

FOREWORD ix

INTRODUCTION xi

The dialogues begin xvii

= Year 2009 = ... 1

= Year 2011 = ... 9

= Year 2012 = ... 34

wd

FOREWORD

This is a stylized journal incorporating my thoughts and comments on Life and the workings of the mind. The ideas came spontaneously and they evolved over many dialogues of varying contexts. The substance of this book is based on my input while participating on an internet Personal Development forum during the three years of 2009, 2011 and 2012.

These thoughts are pointers on a journey of awareness, hopefully leading to clearer understanding, which can be somewhat complex to define.

The words came almost automatically with very little "mental composition". When I think about it now, it surprises me and at the same time there is no real surprise.

Now I invite you to share in my particular exploratory adventure of watching thoughts.

walt

~.~

wd

INTRODUCTION

I don't know how to think. DO YOU?

How does one THINK?

Do you squeeze your eyes shut, tighten your entire body and will a thought into being? What are the mechanics of thought?

Or do thoughts just happen? Are they just there and over the years we develop an ability to attach to them in some way. And then do the thoughts become "my thoughts" and "her thoughts" and "their thoughts"?

But if thoughts just happen, then where do they come from?

Some would say that 'you' think. If that is so, then how would you think to stop thinking? After all, if you are the one in control of those thoughts you call yours, then shouldn't you be able to stop them at will?

Go ahead. Stop thinking. What will you do? Shout in your mind "STOP!" or "SHUT UP!". But those are still thoughts. That is thinking. It hasn't stopped.

All of this is happening, and yet someone (something or some nothing) is seeing all this as it happens.

You are actually witnessing it in real time. So you cannot be the thoughts that you are witnessing, for they appear to be other than you.

So whatever sees thought cannot be thought.

So I cannot be a thought, or can I? If I am my thoughts, then in who's mind are these thoughts? Or does that even make sense?

Pushing this a bit further a question of identity arises.

Who, or what am I? – What is this "I", or "me" that we feel so attached to or a part of?

What are thoughts in essence?

Why do they exist at all?

BUT, I can WATCH them!

I can watch thoughts!

Give it your attention. You can observe or witness the very movement of thought. You can 'see' that flow of energy.

Where are you looking from?

EVERYWHERE! We are non-local beings. Modern day quantum physics confirms it!

So is thought everywhere also? What are the implications here?

Pierre Teilhard de Chardin, a priest, a scientist and a spiritual visionary wrote several inspiring books both scientifically and spiritually based. He lived in the early twentieth century. Two of his outstanding books were the Phenomenon of Man – a scientific treatise on the evolution of humankind and its destination to what he called the Omega Point. Here he introduces the NOOSPHERE, an encompassing sphere of knowingness, intelligence and *'beingness'* that surrounds the planet and all of humanity.

Teilhard de Chardin makes the statement in this book that most people falsely assume we are humans seeking a spiritual or divine experience. But Chardin stipulates that the opposite is the case. We are spiritual being having a human experience.

His other outstanding book that I very much appreciate is "Le Milieu Divin" or "The Divine Milieu". This book is written from a strongly spiritual perspective, (de Chardin was a Roman Catholic Priest), and de Chardin unmistakably includes humanity in the overal picture of divinity.

Burt Harding (a current day 'seer') clearly explains in his book "Hiding in Plain Sight", that there appears to be a dual nature to our existence.

We are human beings. The part that we are mostly accustomed to experiencing is the HUMAN part. That has been the source of our strong conditioning in a phenomenal world. This phenomenal world, through conditioning processes, has become our "reality". In this phenomenal world we experience the opposites or duality of pain and pleasure, good and bad, right and wrong, and various other mind/thought and sensation related experiences. The HUMAN part of us appears to be 'blessed' or 'cursed' with the experience of Life.

But then there is the other part of human being. The BEING part. The BEING that we are is rarely considered. It is in the realm of the spiritual. BEING is related to the verb TO BE. The present tense of the verb TO BE is I AM.

Somewhere, therein, lays the answer to our "beingness" and relationship to Life. Everybody has "I AM" in common. We all use the present tense of the verb TO BE. We are that which IS.

So is this all just thought? Or, can there be a 'seeing' or a perceiving beyond thought into the very nature of being?

Can we transcend the inundation of the captive domain of thought?

We always seem to be identified with thoughts such as I AM hungry, I AM hurt, I AM lonely, I AM important, I AM such and such or I AM great, or I AM unimportant and so on.

Do we ever stop at "I AM" ... not I AM this or that, but simply I AM. That is the basic statement of BEING. That is in the deepest essence who we all are. It is not definable.

This "I AM" can, of course, be a mere thought. But can one just feel the essence of it and not the thought of it?

Then, do I still THINK it – the "I AM", the "BEINGNESS" of what I am?

Many people might say "that I think it", or that "we think thoughts".

But that makes no sense. What really *is* thinking?

I watch the workings of Thought. Thought tells its own story.

Let's see what tales thought will tell about Life. I almost said "My" Life.

But what is mine about it?

I can perhaps call the experiences that I have in that *one* life mine.

But can I actually claim that I am Life? Perhaps! But that is a bit deep for simple explanations right now.

So I take this trip into the domain of thought ... and perhaps beyond...

And thus the tale begins...

~.~

The dialogues begin...

The online dialogues began in April of 2009 when I joined a forum for discussions on Personal Development.

My interests were not really in the area of the topics that were being casually discussed by the participants of this forum.

There were some very knowledgeable members who often posted in their areas of interest. Often the remarks were in specifically personal areas of interest. The exchanges between members were played out against a background of basic personal development principles and the forum site owner kept discussions "on-track" and provided articles he had written based on many years of experience in the field of Personal Development. He was a fan of Tony Robbins – a personal development guru.

It is in this environment that I began to probe the members for responses that might reach beyond the commonly popular level of engagement in discussing the area of personal development.

It was not as easy a task as I had first envisioned, but gradually several members started to respond to my probing.

The rest of this book is recorded in a journalized style. I extracted the things that interested me most and have recorded entries herein from my personal perspective.

The journal entries begin with entry number one in April of the year 2009. This entry is titled *April (i)*, identifying it as the first entry in April. *April (ii)* would be the second entry in April, and so on. This notation records a sequence of events rather than dating them specifically.

= Year 2009 =

April (i)

What is "the self"?

Am I "in a rut"? How do I get "out of a rut"?

Have you been in that sort of place before? More than once? Maybe?

At least maybe you have an inkling or 'suspicion' that perhaps you have been "sliding into a rut" somewhat on a regular basis. Or maybe you have noticed some sort of pattern to some undesired behaviour.

Maybe you can you see that there is a 'habitual' pattern, that has become almost like some boring routine of life. Or maybe some particular behaviour keeps repeating over and over – and it's not helping you to 'grow' – to evolve. Do you get the feeling that you may have some sort of limitation, something is inhibiting your further flowering or maturing into the greatness you might be hoping for?

If you can sense anything in the above statements that might even remotely apply to your life situation, then maybe some "personal development" would be useful for your intellectual enlightenment.

The astute observer of personal mental processes and habits, can see the kind of "world" they are creating around themselves for their personal experiencing.

Basically the above is the preamble to a dialogue we can begin within ourselves, on the matter of the 'next phase' of personal development.

This would be an approach that is somewhat different from the standard concepts of personal development as used in the everyday industry of "self help".

In what way could we dig a little deeper into understanding ourselves and how we create our own limitations and problems?

Why do we fall into habitual patterns of behaviour that tend to retard our progress and accomplishments?

Could the ancient adage on the temple entrance at Delphi "Know Thyself" have any import to personal development?

There may also be other questions to consider regarding the 'Next Phase' of personal development.

It would be useful to engage others in conversation about ideas and experiences that might evoke some useful personal insights. There is a certain synergy that evolves from such combined participation. Such a shared approach, with its synergistic momentum may contribute in most unexpected ways to our personal development.

~.~

April (ii)

Could the next phase of human development be a product of the workings of human nature or instinct? The questioner supposes that human nature or instinct is a 'great composite of genetic inheritance, societal influence and the basic quest for survival...

My response...and further inward cogitation... follows:

So are you then posing the separation of nature (be it human nature or all nature) and what we have called self?

Is not the 'intellectual' self in essence a product of thought which *is* the result of "that great composite of genetic inheritance, societal influence and basic quest for survival" as you put it?

Thus my question -"...who is it (or what is it) that displays this pride, vanity and the rest of that sort of thing?"

My question is intended to lead towards the investigation of that intellectual self. This 'self' that we have personalized (given a personality to), which now behaves as an entity in separation from the whole.

We call ourselves individuals, meaning undivided, whole (=holy), complete, etc.

And yet, we seem to be quite separate and *separative* in our behaviour.

But if there is a 'self' that considers itself to be separate from other 'selves':

If that is true, then should we not look into this carefully?

Should we not observe more deeply?

Should we not find out something important like:

"Why is there a lack of harmonious existence amongst humans on this planet?"

~.~

April (iii)

"self " - The temporal ruler of the mortal domain we experience in life.

The one that preoccupies us so much in youth.

And hopefully, this 'self ' learns how to yield to greater understanding and appreciation of life.

A yielding that welcomes the dawning of wisdom which transcends 'self ' and welcomes the eternal.

~.~

April (iv)

If we cannot learn from what we think and say – then all the personal development in the world is useless. A quote my spouse often sends my way:

"Life isn't as serious as my mind makes it out to be."

And a quote that I particularly take to heart with some deeper understanding:

"I don't mind what happens to me." (J. Krishnamurti explained this to be his "secret").

Let's not leave out William Shakespeare's reminder from the play *Hamlet* :

"There are more things in heaven and earth ... than are dreamt of in our philosophies."

So, if you can allow the above into your personal play of life, you will have lost nothing!

And perhaps you will gain that illusive treasure of freedom.

Not freedom 'from', nor freedom 'to do' something – but supreme FREEDOM itself. No more bondage, no more loss, no more worry. – To be! – I am – .

~.~

April (v)

Can we consider self and ego to be manifestations of thought?

Here is a train of thoughts that I am watching now:

- We have experiences in Life.
- They are stored in memory.
- The recall of that memory in motion = thought.
- Thought/intellect does not want to feel alone.
- Thought/intellect wants to be noticed! It must have comparison.
- Relationship: to experiences, environment, self and others.
- Thought/intellect seeks recognition and so it invents a personality (ego, self).

> The Importance of ego/self is evaluated by thought constantly.
> This leads to the formation of a psychological 'image' of self
> Any attacks on such image are usually strongly defended by thought
> Thought feels it must defend the image it has created of self
> If it doesn't protect the image then the image can be lost
> Loss of image = 'death' = fear
> and fear is the beginning of various phobias
> and this leads to further need for protection *of what I 'think I am'*.
> It is still all thought.

This can get very involved.

Freud, Maslow, and many other intellects have written hundreds of books on this activity of thought/mind. But most people will never get to read what the 'analysts' had to say about all of this.

Therefore, how does one find out?

One's own opinion, or even another's opinion? Opinions are obviously products of thought! All opinions are merely expressions of thought, and thus they are limited.

<u>Thought as opinion</u> can only provide 'opinionated' answers and not an answer that is unbiased. Thought will always include some sort of bias.

Now another view has been hinted (a higher Self). And there is much literature about that also. But how did such a thought enter our consciousness? That in itself could be very interesting.

It has been said that a problem created at a certain level cannot be solved on the same level (I paraphrase Einstein, of course).

All-in-all, if we are limited to discuss only what atheists will accept, then it will be a very superficial coverage of this subject.

I do not include children in this. There are ways to talk about various levels of understanding with children. Children can quickly grasp things beyond the fixed, limited, intellectual attitudes of the adult mind.

Children have had less exposure to conditioning. They are freer to see 'deeper' in their own way. When we 'explain' it to them and tell them what is 'real' and what is 'fantasy' as if we really know everything, then we begin to condition them to the adult point of view.

Teaching children without introducing erroneous beliefs is a delicate matter.

It takes a Master's touch.

~.~

= Year 2011 =

August (i)

It has been said that it is insane to argue with what is.

Well, one can argue with what is, but then one will suffer as a consequence.

If it is within one's means to change what ***is*** to improve a situation then this could be considered an intelligent action, however, if there is no possibility nor probability in changing what ***is*** (e.g. rainy day, broken foot, etc.), then it is wisdom to acknowledge what ***is*** without inner mental argument.

Understand that whatever ***is*** can never imperil nor threaten the essence of what you really are. Therein lays a hint to the "Kingdom of Happiness".

~.~

August (ii)

I caught my thoughts executing an old conditioned negative cycle of justification etc.

Attention alerted me to the mischief that thought is capable of starting.

This mischief can cast our life scripts into scenarios of havoc.

Stopping *thought* dead in its tracks brought a knowing smile of joy to my face and heart.

-o-

I must clarify that you cannot stop thought permanently (unless perhaps when your body dies – then there is no longer a brain to receive the thought energy information). However you can momentarily "stop" thought in its tracks in the sense that thought ceases to have an impact on you. You no longer react to the impulses of undesired thoughts.

The moment that you are aware of thought in relationship to your behaviour then thought no longer has an impact. You, the deeper sense of you, not the thought-directed you, are then truly "present" and aware "in the moment".

~.~

August (iii)

Regarding LOVE: It has been said that 'love' is seeing yourself in another. That does not refer to the 'egoic self' but rather that Self that is common to all.

Regarding Life and Death: People in general understand death to be the opposite of life, but as many ideas that make up our understanding the usage of language is not a very accurate conveyor of actual experience. Also, lacking understanding of any matter, one is likely, through habit (conditioning) to accept an explanation by an '*authority*' they trust, and end further enquiry into the matter.

Looking more closely we can see that what we generally call the experience of human 'life' is the period extending from BIRTH to DEATH. Those are the two extremes of our earthly experience, and following the rule of opposites as we have defined them in our society (dualistic mind), the opposite of Death is Birth.

From this one can note that the span of Birth-Death is but a 'fleeting moment' in the 'stream of consciousness' called Life, and Life has no opposite in actuality. We can invent a term called 'non-life' and call it the opposite of life, but then that is just a convention of language. Even when an organic life form 'dies' there is no non-life, because what follows the physical event we call death is a decomposition of matter and a 'transformation' into other 'forms of life'.

Thus in the entire continuum, there is only life and we humans have in that continuum artificially demarked (set the boundaries) for the expression of a 'form of life' as the period between the events of birth and death. We could make an analogy to help understand this topic of birth-death in relationship to the 'stream of consciousness' called life.

We could picture it like this (sort of a parable-or metaphor):

There are two portals (doorways, gates). One portal has a sign above it which says **BIRTH**. The other portal has a sign above it labelled **DEATH**.

The 'stream of consciousness' is always in action, moving everywhere. There is a movement of awareness in that 'stream of consciousness' entering through the portal called **BIRTH**. Consciousnes individuates (takes on separate forms of manifestation) at BIRTH. This consciousness then proceeds to enter a stream of manifestation called "life events and experiences". That stream of experiences in consciousness appears to last for a short interval (sometimes up to 90 years or so). After this interval of experiencing, the vehicle for this phase of experiencing (i.e. the body) disolves, dies. With this phase of experience completed consciousness exits by another portal – **DEATH**.

The awareness of the 'stream of consciousness' that we call Life continues. It has no beginning and no end, and we as a collective totality along with the entire universe are that awareness moving in 'the stream of consciousness'.

Therefore, to answer the questioner(s), one would say NO, not afraid of death, because there is an understanding of what Life really is.

If there is fear it would be the 'egoic sense of self' expressing fear due to its attachment to limited concepts or ideas of life and death.

Once there is an insight into what the egoic self actually is, then the nature of the real Self comes to light. Then one is free of all fear and at peace about everything.

~.~

August (iv)

The human mind has played a game for a long, long time.

The game is called LET's PRETEND.

What the game amounts to is the creation of a world built with thoughts, with explanations or definitions of what everything is. This provides a feeling of security in a world designed by concepts.

We have a parallel example in what we know as our physical world. There we also use thought and concepts to 'create' the structures (buildings, roads, bridges, cars, airplanes, etc) that seem to confirm the reality of physical existence. Even when we dream the mind continues to create all sorts of conceptual worlds. The same is true when authors write wonderful fiction stories.

But these worlds are all conceptual worlds - worlds of the mind.

And is not the physical world in which we find ourselves also a conceptual creation?

If you create your world based on definitions or perceived meanings and acquired mental conditioning, how can you be certain of anything real? Everything in your world is then derived from possibly quite erroneous mental processes, ideas and definitions. These might approximate reality but ideas, concepts or definitions can never reveal what is real. That can only be realized through direct experience.

It is a very shallow existence when one always makes reference to how something is defined to be by an 'authority' of some sort. Definitions have their place. They are useful in practical daily applications when we need a consensus on communicating and sharing ideas with other people in many circumstances (engineering, medicine, teaching, giving directions, etc.)

The ever present 'danger' in accepting definitions as an arbiter is that one is soon conditioned to expect a 'pat' answer for any question – just refer to the 'authority' on that subject and you *'know-it-all'*. Often we have to discern deeper implications and nuances that are not discussed in the provided 'authoritative' definition.

Life is not a matter of definitions, but a matter of living and experiencing.

~.~

August (v)

Many people fear Life.

If one looks at it very closely it still amounts to the fear of death.

Life to the intellectual mind is an idea/concept.

The mind (thought) can only understand in terms of ideas, or concepts, and fears to give up any of those beliefs. Why does it fear? The evolutionary process has honed the survival instinct to a very high level of priority.

This survival instinct, which upon which the body depended in the early millenia of evolution in no longer a great necessity for the further evolution of man. In fact, it has proven itself to be an impediment to civil development.

Now let us consider why many people fear Life as much as Death.

We can observe expressions of life and go through experiences in life of which we can have an intellectual understanding. Thus life in its essence involves direct experiencing. Egoic thought (egoic mind) feels that it must retain authoritative control of its understanding of life, and this position from which the egoic mind possessively operates is only a conceptual reality. Living strictly by means of mind is like computer gaming in a virtual reality.

Death is also an idea/concept that the mind formulates on its own terms of perceived survival needs. In fact, having evolved through millennia of witnessing that which has been called death, the egoic mind would rather not entertain concepts that would seem to deny its continued existence. Therefore there is fear of death for the obvious reason of perceived self extinction. There is also the fear of Life because from its place of conceptualizing everything, mind does not really know about Life other than its *theories* about life.

Thus it would seem that to understand life is to understand death. Since the mind will never be able to understand either it displays behaviour in terms of fear of life and/or fear of death.

Fear of "dying" appears to be different from fear of death. Death is the unknown but dying is a progressive process that brings one closer to death every moment. Dying is at least something the conceptual mind can grasp through experience up to the actual point of what is called death.

Of death the mind can have no experience, because once that portal has been entered the mind no longer has a body to function through – no brain and no organs of perception.

~.~

August (vi)

What is happiness?.

What I call true happiness occurs in moments when there is no actual thinking occurring. It sometimes appears as a momentary feeling of being free, uninhibited, at peace, and there is an absence of stress and sometimes as all these feelings combined appear in the context of happiness.

Whenever I became aware of how happy I '*was*' it became a *past* experience, and that feeling of happiness dissipated.

In a sense I feel that happiness is a 'happening' or a 'being' event that we experience. It is not a permanent state. When we try to 're-live happy moments' by thinking about them and then try to recreate the feelings and conditions for that happiness to happen again, it does not manifest - because now it has become a mental effort of the ego/intellect.

When true happiness was manifesting there was no ego, nor intellectual processes in action. There was sort of a 'forgetting' of all that. The 'false' self is dropped away naturally and the real 'Self' IS. These moments might perhaps be labelled as *'moments of heaven'*.

What I wish to convey is that manufactured, or conceptualized, or theorized happiness is *not* happiness. Therefore any study about it is just theory and more spinning of the 'intellectual wheels'.

~.~

August (vii)

Are you spiritual?

To the Intellectual mind the answer will always be an opinion based on cultural conditioning or belief (which is just a way of thinking).

....What does spiritual mean?

The obvious answer is "Check the dictionary." Other than that, "What do you want it to mean?"

Is there a hidden desire or hope in the back of your mind for some sort of fulfilment or of improving your undesirable life experience?

Are you living a life of meaning?

This sort of question is one of desperation, hoping that a usable answer is available to make the intellect/ego less fearful of the uncertainty of its experience in life, about which it has no comforting idea.

An answer to consider is that perhaps you as 'ego/intellect/thinking personal self' really have no power nor understanding of what is being asked here.

'Life is its own meaning', but of course the intellect will never buy into that. It wants an answer that will please itself, make itself happy. The ego/intellect seeks help in understanding. "Please tell me what to do", it begs. It wants some source to say to it " *If you do a), b), and c), then you are a good person, and you are assured a place in 'heaven' ".*

That is the problem of ego/intellect as it manifests in mankind. The egoic mind developed the power of conceptualizing which ensured improved the abilities for survival. This was a definite benefit and need for the species to survife.

However, when survival was made more secure, based on the abilities provided by conceptualization, mankind started to fall into an almost naturally occurring belief that he/she **are** the thoughts that they were thinking. Careful inquiry into one's own mentality will demonstrate that thought/intellect is always limited and prone to error.

So what is a human being?

We do not mean the physical, thinking organism here. Look into it with some earnestness about really wanting to find out. The 'finding out' will not be a matter of memory or thought.

Who is it that is aware that one is thinking a thought, when it happens?

Why do thoughts cross our awareness and seem to appear from the 'nothingness of the what' and soon return thereto?

Usually we latch onto a thought and become attached to it to the degree that we start to believe that it is our thought and we are thinking it!

Man's delusion and problem in life could be summarized as "Lost in Thought". That is a quote from Eckhart Tolle and seems to fit quite well when we observe the state of the world (especially recently).

~.~

August (viii)

What comes forth from the 'mind' (i.e. thought) is always relative and most unreliable in understanding the whole. We can notice that any concept coming forth from mind – such as a concept of 'value' - is relative and personal and can just as quickly turn around to be the opposite on another occasion.

That is the nature of dualistic perception. All concepts are limited and therefore cannot logically bear the name 'truth' - which to the mind is another concept.

Thus humans continue to be "lost in thought" as long as they believe that they are a body or the authors of the thoughts observed by awareness.

~.~

August (ix)

Beliefs are simply thoughts or ideas that have been repeated enough times to become an ingrained habit of behaviour. Beliefs are simply particular kinds of thoughts that motivate a person to behave in a certain way.

There is nothing holy or sanctified about any thought/belief.

Beliefs are useful at certain stages of life, and can become very limiting to 'personal growth' or even 'spiritual growth'. If one is 'stuck' or limited by a particular concept, thought or belief, then the path to a 'deeper' understanding of who we are in actuality is also blocked or limited.

For example, the belief in 'Santa Claus' or 'Sleeping Beauty' is useful in helping children to learn certain aspects of behaviour in society. But once the child matures beyond fairy tales, those beliefs can only stifle further development.

An early belief in our world was that the earth was flat. But that proved to be a huge falsity. So we can see that the mind/ego/intellect is easily swayed by what is called belief.

In understanding belief we take possibly the first step towards a more sane existence.

Regarding the belief that one can "direct" "one's" life:

- Is it even possible to "direct one's life"?

- and, there is certainly life, but can one honestly say that it is "your life"?

- who is this entity that call's itself 'I' ? It often brags "I AM". What is all *that* about? Not the bragging, but the I AM business?

You can say I AM John, Mary or Bill. I AM a lawyer, a carpenter or a teacher. If you think about it carefully, you – YOU not your thoughts of who you think you are – but YOU, cannot be a "something" such as a lawyer or teacher. Those are things you DO, or roles to play.

And when you say I am John, or Mary and so on, you are indicating how you prefer to call yourself or how you would like yourself to be identified, but those are all thoughts ABOUT you. They are NOT YOU.

YOU are what is aware of all these things. YOU are the I AM part of this things.

Who ARE you? The short answer is – I AM. (period!). I am is the present participle of the verb TO BE. This then resolves itself into understanding yourself to be BEING.

"A BEING" at a normal level of understanding, but just "BEING" at a deeper level of understanding.

~.~

August (x)

Regarding the issue of *"HAVE and HAVE NOTS"*:

The ego loves to compare, to see where it stands on the scale of importance, and how it can add more to itself and "puff itself up" so-to-speak.

In the ever-continuing mental activity of comparison there will always be something that someone has that you do not have and might want.

"Have and Have-nots" in essence is one of those non-sense (not sensible) phrases that describe a sorry state of human consciousness - always grasping to get something more, to fulfil oneself, to feel more loved, more wanted, or more meaningful.

You already are all **that** and more! - But the human mind/ego is not to be convinced of this. The YOU that we are talking about is the very awareness of what one calls 'my life' and is common to all phenomenal expressions of life. It is the YOU of unity and 'oneness' rather than the **you** of individuality. The ego wants an identity quite separate from that. ONENESS suggests no individual personality such as ego.

This of course suggests the 'death' of the ego as the independent separate authority of its *separate* life. This ego, is in essence an illusion of thought to begin with.

~.~

August (xi)

If you believe in Santa Claus or the Tooth Fairy, or that the Earth is Flat, then possibly that is exactly what you will see from your perspective.

You may see yourself as happy and confident, and it may manifest *'on the surface'*, but it only promotes an illusion along with the many existing illusions of self that are ferociously defended by thought/ego.

'Seeing' supersedes the need for believing. Whereas belief is a habitual way of thinking about something, 'seeing' implies removing the veil of illusion put up by erroneous thinking in the first place.

Thus through careful introspection one could see the true value of what beliefs are and transcend the limiting thinking of the ego/intellect and arrive at the joy of living.

~.~

August (xii)

"*Think Better*" - by whose standard?

This sort of 'guidance' is very misleading and can sometimes lead to faulty beliefs in one's own "improvement".

Within *the mind* ego wages an endless battle. It is a barrage of *unrelenting thoughts* to become better, to be loved, to be respected, to be a somebody, and so on.

You already are a somebody!

"Think Better" implies comparison, effort, stress and possibly depression if one consistently fails to live up to expectations. What you really are is beyond thought. *Thinking better* can improve functioning on the superficial level of life, in the workplace, and so on. But, thinking better can also create stress if you believe that you unable to think better. See yourself, "YOU" as the witness of thought, not the thinker of thoughts – and then see what happens.

Be inspired today!

Certainly, but it cannot be put as a command! Inspiration does not spew forth from thinking or even from "Thinking Better". Relax into being the awareness that you are, and watch the miracle of life happening. That is the beginning of inspiration. Inspiration comes from root words that literally mean "to breathe in" . The word *inspiration* could also be looked at as *in-spiration* and with a little twist of lettering **in-spirit** *(+ a on)*.

The word inspiration comes from the late Latin *inspiratio*, and derives from the past participle of the verb *inspirare*, «*to blow into or upon; to breath into*» formed by the verb *spirare* «*to breath*» . In the Christian Bible it is used in the sense of the basic meaning "God-breathed".

To 'inspire' is to breath in. To 'expire' is to breathe out. Often the term 'He/she has expired' is used in the case when a body 'dies' to indicate that the last **_out-breath_** has been made.

To uncover a clearer understanding of 'inspiration' as it is used here, perhaps a closer look might lead one to comprehend that inspiration is that which transcends any sense of thought. A certain train of thought may follow inspiration but if one's mind is occupied with thinking of how can I get inspired with various formulas and ideas for becoming inspired, then it is not going to happen.

Inspiration, springs forth, when there is freedom from thought.

~.~

August (xiii)

Re: Altruism and other 'ism's and belief systems

A careful look at any 'ism' will soon reveal that we are dealing with a product of mind, based on conditioned ideas of hope and how to make life 'right'.

This cannot be done through thought. We can judge life if we want to, but that just puts us at odds with life. One person or even one million persons cannot change the behaviour of the entire population of the world just by thinking it.

Communism is another one of those 'isms' that originally set out with high ideals of bettering the life of mankind, particularly the working class.

Thought is limited. Long-time conditioned conceptual systems reign the human mind. These conceptual systems of the mind cannot be changed successfully, long-term, by another set of concepts. That will just put you back into the same thought system. It's like leaping "out of the frying pan into the fire".

An example: one set of concepts eventually formulated Communism. The original concepts did not seem to be working as hoped for. (The limitation of thought is evident in this sort of thing).

To force the desired results (another limitation of ideation), an "elite" group of "*politicos*", led by Stalin and others applied a new set of concepts in hopes of creating the perfect communist state.

Once again, the limitations of thought became very evident as the complexion of Communism as a movement radically changed and entered a realm of insanity.

It became a movement run by a small group of basically 'insane' people. It is one of the greatest examples in history of ego/intellect in action in hopes of finding a 'cure' for social problems and ending up with a nightmare which included the murder of over 10 million people and the establishment of the totalitarian state which we have known as the Soviet Union.

Approach any ideology with caution.

No! Actually better than that - **avoid** all ideology.

Ideologies are products of limited thought. Thought does not 'know it all' and what is conceived by thought can always be added to and corrected. That is how we know that thought is limited and should always be used with caution.

It is much safer to observe the movement of thought and from the revelations of those observations proceed with whatever inspiration reveals itself in moments of silence.

If one wishes to be truly free in the deepest sense of the word then one must understand the consequences of attachment to ideas, ideologies, 'isms' or anything for that matter.

~.~

August (xiv)

It seems that some 'hot spots' have been touched by the word 'religion' and related belief systems.

If one would firstly observe that all beliefs are actually thoughts that have been repeated enough and conditioned to the point of habitually determining how an individual behaves, then one might get a different appreciation of what all of this is about. Different cultures have evolved, various belief systems in isolation from other cultures, for specific reasons that can be discussed in detail at length. But this would be very difficult to do effectively and in depth in an online forum format.

It can be logically demonstrated how thought works to create various dependencies, phobias, and illusions about life. These items alone, have been the source of the fields of psychiatry, psychology and moral philosophy.

When one chances to enter the field of organized religion as an orientation of life style, then depending on the depth of personal attachment, the logic system of thought may be used to what seems to others as total delusion sometimes.

Religions and beliefs of any sort can be totally logical. As many of you know, logic is simply a specific type of formalized thought process.

The human intellect reasons in basically two ways. Inductively and deductively.

An inductive thinker is more likely to 'invent' a religion than a deductive thinker. However, those who accept a religion or any belief system, do it through the deductive process of thinking.

Deductive reasoning always starts from a premise. For example the premise could be "There is a God who created everything and knows everything and is all powerful, and we are his children". This would be the major premise for the intellect to begin with.

The intellect can reason _logically_ from that point onwards. Even if the original premise is patently false, the process of reasoning that stems from it is considered to be totally logical (as far as that premise is concerned).

That is how logic relates to thinking. So, the next time that you feel that your reasoning is logical, have a close look at the original premise from which all that thinking stems, and that will give you a very good idea as to whether you wish to continue with that belief structure or re-consider the criteria of your premise.

As long as people strongly believe in something and do not inquire deeply into the mental process that brings about their belief, they will suffer for it in one way or another, and live in delusion.

Even the atheist faces the same problem. The atheist's problem is that they believe their logical reasoning to be soundly based on their premise, which may be totally false to start with. Like everyone else who talks about a divinity, the atheist does not for a fact know that there is not a divinity. In a sense then even atheism can be thought of as a religion. It would then be a religion of believing in the human form manifestation, natural evolution, and what some scientists believe and tell them. There is perhaps still hope for divine revelation for those people who do not take the atheist's limited point of view.

Just something to consider, 'run with it' or leave it. In either case, what IS does not depend on the meagre ruminations of an inflated human intellect/ego.

~.~

December (i)

"TRUE MEANINGS"!

TRUE and Meaning are both very tricky. Wars have been fought over "True Meanings" or the so-called "Truth". Anyone who cares to jump on the bandwagon of "what is TRUE" is bound for excitement of one sort or another.

As a very potent Chinese proverb says "May you live in interesting times".

The rest of the world did not know what that proverb meant for a long time, but now many people have learned that it is actually a beautifully constructed curse!

"What is the True meaning of ..." ANYTHING?

If this is tackled strictly from a mental perspective (i.e. MIND/EGO/THINKING) then one ends up with either clever philosophical or religious argument, or possibly an incitement to conflict of one sort or another, depending on what that ANYTHING happens to be.

The realm of thought is often inseparable from opinion, which then leads to "my opinion versus your opinion or else ...".

Where there is TRUTH can there exist any possibility of argument? Well, thought will always argue. It is the nature of ego to want to be right and to make someone else wrong. That is how it maintains its energy for survival and its illusion of separateness from everyone else.

If a TRUE thing were "to stare someone in the face" so-to-speak, would one even be able to formulate words (which require thought) and exclaim that this is the Truth. There may be creative ways, beyond the limited scope of simple thought, such as poetic or mystical sayings – but to try to define or explain such would only lead to conflict with someone or other, sooner or later.

Those who have really had that encounter "*of the beyond*" kind and thus have come "face-to-face" with the "*unspeakable*" would not venture to make such a silly statement of "The TRUE meaning of ...".

This whole matter touches on compassion and understanding that is always beyond the realm of thought.

~.~

December (ii)

Every person's story is in some deep sense a reflection of our own story.

The culture,
the background,
the gender,
the experiences,
and all the other descriptors that are possible for another human,
may be different from what we think of as our own being.

But deep down,
at the level of the heart (the spiritual core of an individual),
the desire,
the yearning,
the search,
the need,
is basically the same.

This "level of depth" is recognizable to anyone
who is not resistant
to facing
without judgement,
what one truly *is*
at the core of one's being.

Deep down there is only beauty
and ugliness is born of thought.

~.~

December (iii)

Quote:

This place is a dream.
Only a sleeper considers it real.

Then death comes like dawn,
and you wake up laughing
at what you thought was your grief.

... Rumi - ("The Dream That Must Be Interpreted")

~.~

December (iv)

A Reminder that points to who we truly are:

This above all: to thine own self be true,
And it must follow as the night the day,
Thou canst not then be false to any man.

Shakespeare (Hamlet)
inspired by Socrates' teachings (Know thyself).

~.~

= Year 2012 =

January (i)

Ultimately all search or "seeking" is for Love. It is the lower case "l" love that is usually associated with pleasure and various emotions. Anything that brings pleasure is mind stuff. The brain/mind evolved on the pain/pleasure principle for survival. Survival is dependent on, amongst other related things, the avoidance of pain and the maximization of pleasure.

When we look at upper case "L" Love, we have entered a different paradigm, a new dimension of perception which is beyond the normal 5 senses and yet includes everything.

Pleasure, or any "mind stuff" is not a pointer to this "L" Love, other than the feeling of yearning or a feeling of lack or separation from the 'oneness' of life. This is usually an unconscious process (or subconscious if one prefers) therefore the ordinary thinking processes never can "catch on".

"L" Love is that dimension of 'being' which transcends thought, emotion and all that other "mind stuff".

That is why many spiritual teachings in various ways point to Love or equate Love to "God, or Spirit, or the deepest core of being".

One example is from the Christian New Testament in - 1 Corinthians 13:3 (NIV) Paul (formerly Saul the tax collector) says:

If I give all I possess to the poor and surrender my body to the flames, but have not love, I gain nothing.

... and some versions translate the end of that quote as

... if I have not love, then I am nothing.

This particular translation goes beyond thoughts usual ideas of 'gain' as translated in the first instance above. The translation into "*... I am nothing*" instead of "*... I gain nothing*" touches upon the "*no thing/every thing*" paradox of the unknown, the ineffable, God.

It points to what one ***is*** in essence. (i.e. *not* the body, not the mind, *not* the things I possess, *not* the things I believe or think about, etc.)

... Thus, in essence, the second translation above subtly supports the idea of us as individuated spiritual beings having a human experience.

~.~

January (ii)

If we consider only the physical *expression* of life to understand life, then we are limiting awareness to a particular belief or opinion.

The physical form changes - whereas life goes on.

The personality seems to dissolve - but then are you the personality? – OR – is the personality merely a tiny by-product of the multifarious expressions of life as we believe to know it?

The question actually revolves around **who** we really ***are***.

Are you the *thoughts*?
Emotions?
personalized memories?
personalized mind (which is thoughts and memories)?
beliefs (which *are* your thoughts)?
are you the *body*?

OR, are we something *more* than just these mere expressions/manifestations of life?

Might not one consider that we are an aspect of Life itself, experiencing itself through form?

Can one fearlessly enter into this sort of deep and very subtle self inquiry? Do you dare to abandon all presupposed beliefs and underlying fears?

If you can do this, enter that depth of "self"-inquiry, you will be amongst and elite, even like unto the disciples of all the masters – Jesus, Buddha, Lao Tsu, and many, many others.

Take the challenge! There are many challenges in life much less worthy of your attention.

Take the challenge of challenges, the journey of journeys.

What is your Life purpose? You will find out. But *not* by embracing thought as a vehicle of knowledge for the discovery of YOU.

Who you are and who you think you are – those are two entirely different paradigms.

> ➤ Who you *think* you are is a process of *thinking* a*bout* an object. THOUGHT projects an object to be realized (made real) in the personalized mind. Thought projects an object *called* YOU. That becomes the object of thought. It is who you *think* you are.
>
> ➤ Who you **are** is an experiential *discovery* taking place NOW. Thinking cannot do. Thinking involves time – yesterday, today and tomorrow. Past and future are projections of thought. NOW is the ever present where thought cannot abide. It is the realm of direct experiencing

Set foot on the true path of discovery.

~.~

January (iii)

It might be more correct to say that humans *believe/think* there is a problem.

Generally speaking "problems" are a product of mind. Those things that demand solutions now, in the moment **may** be called problems, but they are actually **challenges** that provide us an opportunity to arrive at a creative solution.

The human brain appears to have been designed to work with what it calls problems, although it would be more correct to say that the human brain evolved to interact with the environment in such a way so as to maximize its survivability.

It appears that often, the human mind even goes so far as to "create" problems so as to "entertain" itself, thus creating somewhat of a "fiction" out of its supposed life. Apparently, for some people this is "exciting".

Just look at the world political scene, or the news any day, and this factor is difficult to overlook. It is part of the "human comedy", or as some would put it "human tragedy".

The human mind often conceives a situation to be "reality". This conceived "reality" is rarely anywhere near the actuality (what actually **is** the case). This has been demonstrated many times over throughout human history. If you wish to confirm this it is not difficult to do so.

~.~

January (iv)

How do you relate to life?

In other words,
how do you see your connection
to the reality
that surrounds you?

Do you feel separate from Life?

Do you feel
life is "out there",
and you are here?

Or, do you feel aware
of an ocean of manifestation,
or galaxies of wonderment?

Do you have the notion
that everything
is happening NOW
and all is presenting itself
as continuous waves
of consciousness?

oOo

Then, how do you feel and relate to what you might call your achievements or lack of them?

How do you see *that* in relation to what you might call **your** life?

Where is your focus in regards to yourself and the flow of life at any moment?

Is it what you achieve in life that is of importance in the *overall picture* of life?

> What you achieve,
> what you make of yourself
> is surely temporal.

> It will only last for a while.
> Even if that be one thousand years,
> it is nothing on the universal scale
> of infinity.

> How will you find out
> about this self
> that you so proudly display
> and defend?

> Is there a different understanding,
> a different approach to life?

Now is always the right time
to find out.

Now is the only time
that matters
- since past and future
can be apprehended
ONLY
in the present moment –
now.

Now is the only reality
of which one can be aware,
because –
Now is the place, space and time
in which you can realize
your presence
in being.

Now is all there *is* –
which in essence
is *you*.

~.~

March (i)

People's continuous preoccupation with things leads to the various mental/emotional problems that they experience in their lives.

There is a building of self-image with hopes and desires and idolizing what they would like to become.

But then there are also 'attacks' on that self-image, attacks which one seems compelled to resist or 'fight off' in order to defend this 'self-image' that is valued so much. Our universe seems to be made of 'things' and thus things gain an unusual place of importance in our perception of life.

Things are thought to be of some sort of importance or value, but in reality all things amount to no absolute value (only relative and temporary values).

Among things are also thoughts, ideas, opinions, philosophies and an entire realm of "make believe".

Yes, there are billionaires. So what! That's what *is*. All of them may actually deserve it.

There are kind people.
There are helpful people. also

There are truly selfless and outstanding exemplars that might be included as guideposts for our own experiencing of life. These sorts are usually overlooked, or ignored in favour of 'dreaming' about being wealthy or important, or whatever.

There appear to be '*things*' that are much more important.

When you leave this plane of existence, the 'things' that have so occupied your life experience cannot follow you.

If you have acquired a name, wealth, importance, property, leadership – whatever, it will not follow where you must go, for that is not a part of what you really are. All these 'things' are only artefacts of a temporary/temporal experience.

Happiness is not a '*thing*'. It is actually of the nature that you are.

If your attention is diverted to things then you will eventually experience a state of unhappiness because your focus is away from what you really *are*.

When the focus returns to the core of your being, then happiness is the natural state of your expression.

> Because then
> you are no longer
> relying on '*things*'
> to fulfil you
> or to bring you
> happiness.
>
> There is no need to achieve
> that which you already ***are***
> at the depth
> of being.

~.~

March (ii)

> We just love stories.
> And that is great!

Some stories instruct, some entertain, while others just seem to float many disjointed ideas.

The strange thing about stories is that most people never realize that what they take to be the reality of what they call their "*personal lives*" is also a story.

Can that really be so?

> It is a most grand story.
> There are many dramas,
> emotional incidents,
> instructional occurrences,
> and often there is a lot of suspense
> (that is, it makes no sense...*non-sense*).
>
> There is love, and hate, and hurt feelings, and the dread of what tomorrow may bring, and also moments of great joy and love.
>
> > The greatest story
> > on earth
> > may be the story
> > of yourself.

In fact it may be the only story which appears in many forms including books and movies and songs and dreams. Maybe we should pay closer attention to the story of ourselves and enter the dimension often mentioned by the world avatars and saints.

As William Shakespeare put it - *the world is a stage and we are actors upon it - so play your part well.*

The person (comes from persona = 'sound mask') is but a small expression of what you really are. *You* are *that* which *makes* the expression of the person possible.

Thus I venture to ask,

"Are the author of – your own story?"

~.~

March (iii)

Original

        – meaning at the origin
        – at the root ...

          that which you are
          at the core of being

This does not mean trying to be different from someone else. Rather it points to the deep knowingness within that there is *that* which can express in a unique way:

        beyond the confines
        of thought - yet able
        to use thought
        masterfully, to manifest
        the most useful expression
        in life –

through one's particular
material, physical form.

"*Where you <u>want</u> to get*"
is how the ego prefers
to view life.

> The egoic mind has a separative,
> self-centred, view of
> the universe. This view is an
> exclusive and fragmentary approach
> to relationship with
> the universe.

> The universe is no exclusive,
> nor is it fragmentary.

The universe includes all life.

If it is the "*<u>wants</u>*" that drive one's understanding of purpose in life, then that sort of limited approach will always mislead and leave one with a feeling of lack of fulfilment, even when you are "rolling" in millions of dollars.

~.~

March (iv)

In general, there has been some misunderstanding about Life.

There is Life, and then there are the manifestations and expressions which we experience *in* that 'stream' of life.

> Life is One.
> There is no
> "my life" and "your life".

There is no separation in Life itself, but the expressions of life appear as separate, individual manifestations. Therefore, I might erroneously speak of as "my life" as if there was a separation from the totality of the one life.

If one really believes the thought that he of she has a separate life from another manifestation in this universe then that is what is adding to the fragmentation of relationship in one's experience of life.

Psychologically – that is to say "within the workings of one's mind" or in one's conception or in thought – a person may feel that they have a separate life.

But what are you separate from?
Do you not breathe the same air as other people,
    - the same air used by the animals and the trees?

And in that breathing, is there not an exchange of molecules of matter between all living things on the face of the earth?

You may be breathing in some substance of your dog's air, and the neighbour's cat's air, and the air of the little girl in India. Within the molecules of the food of your meals are contained the atoms of elements that were literally forged in dying suns (the stars) many millions of years ago. This is verified by the scientific knowledge of today – not the superstitions of yesteryear.

> There are many manifestations
> and apparent experiences
> of the *one* life;
> but life is a unitary whole.
>
> Popular opinion is always
> a limited and temporal
> view of life.
>
> The mindset of self appears to be
> instant gratification.
>
> That seems to be
> the nature
> of our current society.
>
> This, however, changes
> as understanding dawns.

~.~

March (v)

Most human minds
are entrenched
in a habitual cycle
of repetitious
conceptualizing

Because of this
they are enslaved
to that particular level
of life experience.

~.~

A radical view of personal development

The term "Personal Development" has been around for a while. I suppose most people have a general idea of what it refers to. Very technical definitions turn most people off, since they do not really care what it means, but what can it do for them. Often the term "Personal Development" is used quite loosely.

Then there are various facets of PD such as building specific skills like:

- ✓ communicating via public speaking
- ✓ conveying ideas clearly through writing
- ✓ improving one's character traits to interact with more appeal in the "business world"
- ✓ overcoming some personal inhibition
- ✓ relating to others with an open mind
- ✓ learning how to present ideas from an appealing perspective
- ✓ etc.

Material such as how to become rich or how do to things better do not really fall under basic personal development. These are more in the category of how to sell an idea. It can be part of the activity one brings into one's personal development, but in themselves, "how to" does not actually develop a person, it merely 'adds to' their knowledge base.

There might be some side effects in terms of developing character traits, or having more material to draw on in speeches etc.

Can you see anything more here?

> The radical view
> on personal development
> that came to mind
> goes something like this:

– What if we were to
understand personal development
as an unveiling and enhancement
of who we are?

> – Taking it from the other end:
>> Who are we? – at the core
>> in depth
>> at the heart – in essence?

We have been conditioned
by environment,
by circumstances,
by society, ...
to believe and accept our life situation in a certain way.

That conditioning is always at the root of how we function in our relationship with the world (people, ideas, everything).

Can we unveil, uncover, gain an understanding to see beyond those conditioned limitations that affect our activity and performance in daily life?

Instead of chasing "cure-alls",
methods, formulas and
the 'X' steps to success (which may work for a time for some),
can we see the truth of what our potential actually is?
– If there is a natural ability or talent within us,
how will we find it or 'see' it?

– And then,
how could we develop or enhance it?

Personal Development

– The discovery and enhancement
    of who we are!

Are you waiting for someone else to define who you are?
        Or, are you ready for the quest
            of discovering who you are?

Introspection,
self-inquiry,
relentless pursuit of the truth of oneself:

These are all key elements
of the radical view of personal development.

And then what will you find?

Will there be a sweetness to life that escapes one in the pursuit and struggle for such things as –

– "success as the world defines it"?
– or 'making your mark'?
– or to become "a somebody"?

You already are a somebody!

What do you really know of the powerful depth of being that is you?
Who will define you?
Who will discover your true potential?

You can look to others for examples,
but in the end,
you must see your place
in the task of personal development.

It will not happen without your insight,
without giving yourself over totally
to finding out
what the truth of yourself *is*.

What is personal development?
Who are you?

~.~

March (vi)

In the field of science any thesis is subject to peer review. Experimental results must be reproducible to be accepted. That is the purported formula.

However, have you considered the biases, politics, various agendas etc. that are included in this process. Ideally it should work. And amazingly, much of the time it does seem to work.

Except in cases such as when the American Medical Association (AMA) puts drugs on a safe list after the "scientific" studies have been done and then about every 10 years that same AMA takes these same drugs off the safe list calling them either deadly or dangerous to health.

Science is a word whose origin root word means knowledge.

Thus scientific method = a knowledge method. Nothing special about that. The logic method of thinking was once touted to be something irrefutable, and in a sense it is. But its use is limited to argument that can be designed to arrive at a desired result (not to uncover any truth). It is a tool used mainly by politicians and anyone else who needs to skilfully manoeuvre an audience into believing some point of view.

With logic one starts with a premise which can be arrived at through inductive reasoning and then proceed via deductive reasoning to a conclusion. The conclusion will always faithfully follow as a result of the premise. But, if the premise is false to start with, then the conclusion itself is false.

In a simple example - if someone using the logic method (also known as the Socratic method), could convince another through inductive reasoning that Socrates was immortal, then that would be the premise for the following logic arguments (or syllogism) - This example is a variation on the opposite view usually appearing in college text books on logic:

Socrates was immortal. (Major premise)
Socrates was a man. (Minor premise)
Therefore, all men are immortal. (Conclusion)

The result is logical, deductively produced.

Logic is only one example of an organized thinking method. It is still used as a basis of argument by lawyers in a courtroom trial. The defence usually argues inductively to arrive at a premise with reasons and examples to demonstrate that his client is a person who is not guilty of the charge laid against him or her.

The prosecution usually starts with the premise that the charged person is guilty based on the evidence gathered by the investigating officers, and then proceeds from that major premise to one or more minor premises which will lead to the logical conclusion that the person is guilty.

So we see that thinking has its methods, its purposes and its limitations, and in the end each person will decide which opinion they will accept.

~.~

March (vii)

I wish to first point out that in this dialogue no one is wrong or right.

Terminology, ideas, words, concepts at the '*normal*' everyday level of comprehension only really applies effectively to matters of technology, engineering, mechanics, etc., where specific physical detail is involved, and there are parts or chemicals that have to be combined in such-and-such a sequence etc. Thus, a process may be done in a way that one might label as right or wrong.

But in reference to a living being?

It would be some misconception to deem a living being to be either right or wrong. They just *are*. <u>*One IS*</u>. There is *being* as in the verb TO BE.

As to the question of using the terminology "my life" in the sense that there are multiple, separate lives – this is a subtle point that is commonly overlooked by most people. It almost amounts to a grammatical error in the use of language.

Everyone has their personal experience. But it is an experience of the '*same* ONE Life". We may call it "my life" and "your life", but in essence we are then referring to the personal experiences that we feel as separate from everything else in the universe (including animals, galaxies, trees and other people).

If one were to look very closely, without the interference of our conditioned concepts, then we might see that the "*me*" which I might consider as a separate individual, is actually just a manifestation of thought (sometimes called the *ego*). It is a separative thought (a thought which gives the feeling that one is separate or disconnected from other people and things). This leads to the illusion of a separate "individual life".

Actually even the word "*individual*" is misleading. If one looks up the origin of that word, one will find that it actually means **undivided** or **NOT DIVIDE**. If one were truly **individual** then there would be no sense of separation from the UNITY of Life. We are all part of ONE Life, and have our personal experiences in that ONE Life. Most of the great philosophers from Socrates, Plato and on to the some of the deepest thinking quantum physicists of today understand this, and have written about it, each from their particular perspective.

However, if the way one perceives life is through mentation and definitions, then this sort of view of life is only an intellectual understanding. In that case one is still really attached to the separative notion of "My Life" and "other lives" which appear to be independent. Everything in Life is dependent on something. No one is truly independent.

The ego always likes to think of itself as different, superior and other such distinctly identifying qualities. If one can 'see' how the mind is always qualifying people into categories and various comparisons, then this would introduce a clarity of insight beyond the intellect.

Finding the right words to discuss this sort of topic is always difficult and words are usually not exact. Words are most often wrong for these purposes.

It would be an advantage to take these words to be only pointers to what might be beyond the concept expressed by the words.

~.~

March (viii)

There is a deception in using concepts to get beyond a concept.

Concepts might be thought of as a medium of mind. Mind is simply a word we use to reference the activity of thought. In the absence of thought there is no mind as an identifiable 'thing'.

Therefore, if I were to give you a word or words that tried to answer a significantly conceptual sort of question, the words would still be unsatisfactory to the intellect because the intellect/ego only looks for something that it thinks has meaning for its own sustenance, or importance (i.e. for the ego's importance or sustenance).

This is a very 'subtle' matter that thought cannot grasp. To get beyond thought and the current concept of *'world and self '*, one would have to deeply, and with serenity, question "What or Who am I?" in relation to everything.

Any answer received by mind would of course be misleading, because that would be the intellect/ego trying to get 'in the back door' so-to-speak, and re-assume its position of authority to confirm its misunderstood "individuality".

We have preconceived notions (fixed concepts/beliefs) as to who we "***think***" we are. But to "***know***" who you are in relationship to Life is in essence a matter completely different and beyond thought and conceptualization.

Perhaps the word 'transcendence' could apply here, but, words are so elusive in these matters and words can only point (hint) in the intended direction.

Perhaps a useful approach would be to enter into a type of empathy with life (because we are one with life).

But then – these are only words.

~.~

<u>March (ix)</u>

Is the answer '**out there**', or, is it already available to you but you are not aware of it?

Why does one try to achieve more and more?
Why is there this striving beyond the necessary things in life?

Can one 'see' when '*enough*' has been achieved and there is no need for more?

Why do people feel that it is important to compare oneself to anything or anybody?

> Why compare:
> ----
> one's standing in life?
> one's abilities?
> one's income?
> one's wealth or lack of it?
> one's health or lack of it?
> one's good fortune or lack of it?
> ----
> Why compare?
> Why should it even matter?

If Personal Development has any importance or meaning at all then it is in the direction of helping one to see their own misunderstandings, shortcomings, and how they relate to others, and life.

So it all boils down to "Who are you"?
Not the "defined", conditioned you.
That, must be realized before you can proceed any further. But, who are you beyond the obvious?

If Personal Development interests you at all, then the above questions must not escape your careful attention.

~.~

May (i)

= MOTHER'S DAY =

On this day, Mother's Day, I wish all the mothers a very happy and enjoyable Mother's Day.

It is not only a celebration of the fact that we were all birthed and nurtured by a caring mother.

But perhaps even more profoundly, it is a celebration in understanding that it is the feminine principle of life that is the "executive" branch of all creation. The male factor is the other branch of creation.

Every 'strong' male is imbued with a healthy dose of the feminine in his manifested character.

It is a tribute to the feminine.

Also, we should carefully note that without a strong influence of the feminine factor to mediate the more aggressive male element in life, there would soon be no stable society, nor a progressive civilization.

The feminine has not only the birthing aspect,
but also the nurturing, caring and compassionate aspects without which no society can survive.

And thus, without turning this into a treatise on motherhood and the feminine,
I wish a very happy and joyous day to all you mothers.

Know that you are loved even if some fail to demonstrate it on other days of the year.

Sooner or later their sensitivity will sharpen to that understanding.

~.~

May (ii)

In the psychological realm it seems that if something is "believed in" strongly then the effects can manifest as a reality. This is a reality in many cases for those who believe unquestionably. There are cases where such belief is helpful and other cases where it is demonstrably detrimental in one's life experience.

Thus, those who believe in medicine (or the 'medicine man') seem to be helped by such. That is where the placebo effect found its reality.

> Humankind,
> as a society or a species
> seems to have
> what might be called
> a 'social' belief structure
> wherein many 'basic things'
> have come to be believed in
> as 'the authority'
> in regards to many things in life.
>
> Amongst these are
> the belief in medicine,
> the belief in people with 'degrees'
> or those in any authority.

> There is also the belief
> in moral values - and so on.

This is beginning to change as humans evolve and begin to question the very nature of belief and *being*.

This will lead to greater sanity amongst humans overall

> Finding out who/what
> we really *are*
> and not who we THINK we *are*
> or what some "authority" tells us
> about our very inner nature.

This is something each one must find out for themselves in their own way.

> Others can point out,
> but you must actually
> do the self-inquiry
> and introspection
> to find out.

~.~

May (iii)

Let us look at what has been often spoken of as the "true self" or the "Self" capital "S", as opposed to "self" small "s".

It has even been phrased as the "heart of hearts" or "the deepest inner core of oneself".

This appears to be a reference to the reality beyond what ordinary conditioned thinking understands.

It is not the intellectual/personality "you".

It is one's spiritual beingness which is the same for everyone.

Life is ONE, there is no separation in what we call "normal" human consciousness.

We seem to live the "dream" that we think is reality.

~.~

June (i)

There are many great, discussions and proposals about evolution and enough believers in such things that it limits any deeper understanding of reality.

All ideas, thoughts, discussions, experiments and theories provide just a relative view of reality. In a sense, these things only confirm a "personal" reality (which is relative) and not a universal, and impersonal view of what actually is.

To step out of the limited personal view one needs to, for a moment, consider that *maybe* the thoughts that appear on the 'screen' of one's mind are just thoughts, not very much different from a movie one watches on the theatre or television screen.

In the particular case of the "Theory of Evolution" there are many who believe it to be the determining reality in life. The name "Theory of Evolution" and the entire content and research that went into the formulation of that theory – all of that *is* of course, based on thought. It is all the product of thought and limited as far as thoughts go.

So why is the force of thought so compelling?

Let us look a little more closely at the specific example of one who 'believes' in evolution as an undisputable scientific fact. How can such a one confirm their belief beyond a 'shadow of a doubt'?

The that would be necessary would be to prove beyond a shadow of a doubt that *that* which is the product of evolution (i.e. the "thinking" person) can comprehend the intention and meaning of evolution (assuming evolution to be a fact). Or put another way: Can the creation comprehend its creator?

If the **first** proof is not attained then anything else is conjecture and limited theory, all of which is biased by conditioned human thinking.

If the human actually evolved from some previous state/process then how can it comprehend that which brought it about? Can a computer or computer program comprehend its creator?

Just because someone called Darwin proposed a theory based on the biased thinking of his own species (imagining it to be superior and therefore capable of judging the place of everything in the universe), that does not in any way prove nor give eminence to the product of his ideation.

Can the creation comprehend that which created it?

Any discussion of such a matter is best relegated to opinion.

Mystifying questions arise from this discussion:

What if the creator is its own creation? What is the purpose then? And would it still be possible for the finite mind to comprehend that which is ineffable?

It has been said that the finite cannot comprehend the infinite. Thinking is finite, and there lays the limitation, and thus speculation.

Consider this: thoughts may be pointers to that which is beyond the grasp of thought.

Can one see the workings of thought from an unconditioned source of mind?

~.~

June (ii)

Are systems, courses, and methods of *"changing yourself to be more"* useful?

In general such things can provide some directions, guidelines and confidence building. It can open a new area of adventure in one's life experience – but there is a caveat to consider.

These methods will help those who are predisposed to that sort of course in their life experience.

If that is the basic underlying "programming" of the individual then even if that individual be a 'drunkard and a moron', these methodologies for making a change in their personal life experience will work.

Otherwise, without that deep inner pre-disposition, even if one were to somehow acquire a great sum of money to fulfil their dreams and desires, they would eventually end up where they started.

Just consider this carefully before jumping to conclusions. It is easy to imagine anything, but if the *'internal driving force'* towards that end is lacking, then what will happen?

~.~

June (iii)

You could say that I am a disciple of Life.
(Disciple=student)

The logic of many arguments is most often based on the assumption that the "mountain" of thought upon which those arguments are built is in some way valid. It is the *evidence* that is supposed to support the argument. That is where the error in logic lays. Every student of logic knows that if the starting premise is false, then the logical process (i.e. deductive logic) will lead to a false result. It is very evident, very logical and conclusive.

However, when the logic is not based on a faulty premise (that could change also) then the concluding argument can be said to be valid - but only relatively speaking (i.e. relative to the limitations of thought).

In absolute terms (that which is beyond thought, complete, total, beyond mere opinion), thought can only comment in a very limited way.

Three interesting statements made by Albert Einstein:
------
1. "Reality is merely an illusion, albeit a very persistent one."
2. "The only real valuable thing is intuition."
3. "A person starts to live when he can live outside himself."

~.~

June (iv)

What is success? How do you define success for yourself? If you live in the Western world, success is often defined by the attainment of what's missing in your life.

In the current climate of our culture, we are conditioned to strive for what we don't have in order to compensate for the emotional voids we carry deep down inside.

The ones who manage to achieve the most are deemed successful.

Many of us are subconsciously pressured into wanting a certain type of "success". This subconscious pressure constantly "pushes" us to reach for the next *best* thing. If we are convinced of the reality of our perceived lack then we try to prove to the world and to ourselves that we are whole and worthy of being called "somebody".

That is what can happen (and does for many people) when you are charmed by the idea of personal success.

~.~

June (v)

For some people there is no meaning or joy in self promotion.

Self promotion is strictly a game of the intellect/ego. If you feel that you have to be noticed, or if you feel the need for personal validation in any area of your perceived life then you will feel that you must do something so that others will recognize your worth.

This is a game you will sometimes play and there is nothing wrong with it since there are billions of people in this world and each plays the game that they are most comfortable with.

But do not fall into the illusion that the game you play is the true reality of you. If you are attentive to what you do, how you behave, what thoughts come across your awareness and see that you are not basically different from others in the "*game*", then there will come a time when the illusion will be transcended. You will be comfortable with who you are. You can still play the game, and it will no longer have the *feel* of desperate urgency. You will be free of attachment to the illusion that thought creates – if you are **watching thought.**

Uplifting others, supporting others, and sharing meaningful life insights is the way that appeals to some. And this also is good - for such people to be available appears to be a blessing to those whose "world" falls apart when their "dreams" crumble.

To specify that any one way is better than another can be very misleading. Looking up to another to lead you to "the promised land" is an error of illusion for others can only point and you must discern whether that way is for you

Have you misinterpreted an intellectual concept? ____ Or, are you free of concepts so that you can intuit through perception?

Remember, when you read articles of how to be successful, how to become better, and so on – all of *that* is an opinion being offered by someone for whom his/her ideas/concepts have worked in some way.

But that does not mean that any of those ideas or concepts will work for you. They might, sometimes – it depends on some specific factors. For most people, this approach does not work.

Even if
you become a "robot"
and try to mimic
a "success formula
in hopes that it will work
for you also
- there will be no intrinsic personal value.

You will be playing a roll that someone else wrote
and you will be missing
the joy
of your own
creation.

~.~

June (vi)

What is all this desire, training and struggle about wanting to be a leader?

Who's definition is of real value?

Obviously, with about 7 billion people on the planet
it would be some kind of stupendous wonder
if everyone were to be a leader.

In a deeper sense everyone is a leader, and a follower
at the same time.

A person may be exemplary as a leader in many needed areas. For example:

> A fire-fighter, policeman,
> school teacher, nurse, medic –
>
> These are all great leaders
> when they carry out their skilled functions
> in serving society in their special ways.

A corporate executive may also be a great leader, when he/she demonstrates their care, guidance and consideration for the people that work for them.

With proper nurturing of the employees, an intuitive leader becomes an even greater leader.

A touch of compassion in his/her daily exchanges with the peons adds immense credibility to the leadership role.

The word leader or leadership is perhaps a misnomer. It is more fitting for the art of war, *general-ship* etc. In that arena there are those who lead by earned rank and those who follow - by design.

> But to extend that concept into
> the social ranks of the everyday world
> is to be misled by authoritative points of view.

Authority has its place - but for the healthy growth and interactions of a society with creative potential, the current meaning of authority has no place at all.

True leadership does have a place in society.

We truly value leadership when it brings us together as a whole.

True leadership, as practiced by every meaningful element of society overcomes fragmentation and through compassion stabilizes trends towards despondency and despair.

Such leadership would be a welcome refreshment in an atmosphere of psychic turmoil as is often experienced on this planet.

Leadership, or a leader, is more than an idea, a concept, and some guidelines.

Leadership is not something someone does, rather it is what one *is* - a leader.

~.~

June (vii)

It appears that there are two types of enlightenment 'games' that are generally played.

1. Intellectual enlightenment is generally the common game that is being promoted by various sources.

2. Then there is the enlightenment which is the 'uncovering' of blindfolds
   which have kept us from 'seeing'
   the reality of the world
   which we experience.

Those 'blindfolds' are generally the conditioning factors
> which include
> cultural and social factors,
> family ties and belief systems,
> and genetic factors.

It may be a shock to find out that in reality we do nothing of ourselves, but that everything in a sense 'happens'.

For example: we did not choose to be born ... most people would agree to this; we do not beat our hearts or do our own breathing. If the decision to keep breathing was left up to our mental processes then what would happen if at some point we get involved somehow, and FORGET TO BREATHE ?

Do we think or do thoughts cross our perception and then we organize them in some way?

There are many mysteries the intellect has not been able to comprehend.

~.~

June (viii)

This is a phenomenal universe. Many things appear to our senses. Have no concern about it, or very soon the intellect/ego will manufacture a fantasy or 'drama' for your "entertainment".

Phenomenon: any state or process known through the senses rather than by intuition or reasoning

------

In other words a phenomenon is anything we hear, see, smell, feel, or taste. I would also add to that list that a phenomenon can be the experiencing of anything we believe to be real as "reality". It is a very subtle point but seems to fit nicely into the "dream" that we appear to live.

>Phenomena are basically "appearances" that we encounter in our experience of life.

>The universe is a phenomenon, so are bodies, people, houses, trees, etc.

>Just observe and be.
>That is the *'being'* part of human **being**.

~.~

June (ix)

It appears that there are more and more examples daily, of a new paradigm that is expressing through the consciousness we call humanity.

Old structures in the world society are falling as new ones are arising.

And the same appears to be happening to each of us personally, within our awareness. We might notice these as very subtle, or not so subtle changes if we are sensitive to *beingness*. This is an example of the ongoing march of phenomenal existence.

~.~

June (x)

If you let "*things*" that you cannot change annoy you, then you are falling prey to circumstances over which you have no control.

What is, *IS*. If it is raining, then all your wishing to the contrary does not change what is, but it could make you feel miserable.

You are not your circumstances.

What appears to happen to you can be viewed as something happening FOR you instead of TO you. Seeing from this FOR perspective, you might understand something in a different way.

When you meet another person, at some deeper level you are meeting yourself.

That other has feelings, desires, needs, dreams, beliefs - just like you do.

You may consider their personality to be annoying
– or whatever

But then what we see in another is only possible because
= IN ESSENCE =
we are seeing something of ourselves
being reflected back to us
through that other person.

Some part of our being is in resonance with them.

There is a resonance, things resonate, as in the case of two acoustic musical instruments of similar resonance properties. When they are in close proximity, the sound produced by one can be "picked up" and resonated in the sound cavity of the other instrument. There are several similar phenomena, such as *harmonics* that can be demonstrated on instruments.

The compatiblity for resonance is a natural state operating in every human being. When you 'see' evidence of similarities to your likes or dislikes, your joys or fears in another person, it is a subtle reflection of yourself. You are meeting yourself. If you are sensitive to this then you will begin to learn more and more secrets about yourself and as a result more and more about the rest of humanity.

Therefore, I ask: "Do we let circumstances, annoy us - define us, etc...?"

Or do we reserve such judgements and consider what *is* this life that I am experiencing this moment?

There is NO EXIT from NOW, from this moment.

Our very existence is validated by conscious awareness of what is happening this very moment.

Otherwise, we may as well be asleep and continue dreaming...

~.~

June (xi)

Do you also like people who do NOT celebrate their victories?

There are likes and dislikes, obviously.
But if that is a guideline that one goes by then there could be some 'tough' experiences
that life might deal out.

Rather than judge by *like* or *dislike* it may be
much nobler and illuminating to oneself if one just **witnessed**
what is happening in one's life experience.

Witnessing is like **watching thoughts** and happenings but not getting personally involved in anything.

Celebrate your victories. But it may be best done 'quietly' with inner joy.
Then, share what you learned by helping those who truly need and acknowledge that help.

To bring the attention of credit to oneself publicly often annoys many people (perhaps unduly) and can make one "a target on a high horse" for some others.

But of course, you are free to follow the course that feels right for you in your particular life experience.

~.~

June (xii)

The "control" factor is always a 'relative' matter.

In essence no one has control over anything in life. It just appears that way sometimes to the egoic mind.

There are times when we experience good, empowering feelings and it appears as though we are in control in our life situation. At those times we have attributed the control to our personal efforts, or charisma, or whatever.

After many such experiences, we establish a belief that we actually do all of that. That we actual can control the outcomes of our life experiences. Then when a situation appears to be totally 'out of our control' panic assaults the intellect/ego.

And thus the battle for self-confidence is played out.

And one of the ways of addressing an onslaught against self-confidence is dependent on how we relate to that which we experience.

One questioner put it this way:
"What really does matter is how we feel about it."

That is a good pointer to where the problem may lay. Look into your feelings. Do some introspection.

~.~

June (xiii)

Positive Attitude vs. Life Problems

- How do we see the world around us?
- Does it pose too many threatening aspects that we are constantly reacting to?
- Do we think that if we look at things with a positive attitude then our life will improve for us?

> What do we mean by a POSITIVE ATTITUDE?

> Can our mind somehow become a positively oriented instrument?

> There can be numerous questions in the realm of POSITIVITY versus NEGATIVITY.

> What do we really understand about all this?

> Have we been taking other people's opinions on POSITVE THINKING? (i.e. the opinions of some authority)

Can we learn about this? Can we understand it better?

Do we really understand our life experiences, why and how we experience life?

Perhaps a closer look at this positive attitude stuff will help.

The emphasis on POSITIVE and POSITIVITY is a fad that has been going on for at least 50 years and more so in the last 25 years.

On the whole, a positive attitude towards Life seems like a good idea. In most situations this sounds quite practical and useful. However, is it a *'role'* that we learn to play and deep down nothing really changes?

Well if the role playing works, why not? Does that mean that it may not work?

Of course it is always much pleasanter experiencing in the limelight of POSITIVITY. But things change, and one's view of what works in a 'positive sense' can always change to a negative.

For example sugar is nice and pleasant to sweeten up some favourite food. This may put one in a positive state. However, too much sugar and there may be a negative effect.

So, the very *same thing* can be positive at one time and negative at another time, or positive in one circumstance but quite negative in another.

For example: A golfer plans a one day golf outing. For the golfer the weather chant would be "Rain-rain, GO AWAY! Do not even think to come this way!" Rain would be a most negative event for this golfer's planned outing.

On the other hand – a farmer, a market gardner – looks out upon the drying land where his crop is struggling to mature for market readiness.

For the farmer, the chant is "Rain-rain, COME THIS WAY! I love you, my crops need you." Rain is a very positive event for the farmer who is waiting to market a healthy, income producing crop.

So from such examples it is easier to understand that the *same* thing –rain in this case - can be either positive or negative, depending on the circumstance. A rain that floods the land would not be positively viewed by most people.

THE DUALISTIC NATURE OF THINGS

When we rely on the dualistic nature of things in our life experience to fulfil us, or to make us happy then we are never certain what the next experience will bring.

Our mind and emotions are dualistic in nature. We react in such a way as to shy away from that which discomforts us and towards that which gives us pleasure. The dualistic nature of the mind and emotions is constantly juggling with good-bad, nice-ugly, rich-poor, positive-negative and so on.

Giving credence to either end of these polarities, can only bring limitations into your life experience.

LIMITATIONS

It is not a positive attitude that will make you happy, or bring you peace in your life experience – not for long. - because, as we have seen, the direct opposite can quickly manifest and confront us just when we are least expecting it.

Possibly, our positive attitude may really peeve the person we meet, if for that person our positive is seen as a negative. ("Different strokes for different folks.")

In actuality POSITIVE THINKING is an illusion the mind creates for itself to feel some comfort - but this illusion actually isolates the mind from interaction with the rest of the world. And if you tend to think that you are your mind then you would feel isolated, or feel as if you couldn't depend on anyone and had to do everything on your own, including maintaining this positive attitude.

Are we missing something?

Could there be a deeper understanding of feeling good, or secure, other than playing with this positive attitude thing?

The mind by its very nature is, in the main, a reactive instrument. Have you not noticed this?

Suppose we put ourselves in the place of a witness. Like in a court room of law. Let's say that we are a witness to a car accident at a road intersection.

We should understand that to be an effective, and truthful witness we cannot in anyway attach our sympathies to either party that is contesting the issue of the accident. We must be <u>detached</u>. We cannot favour anyone, for any reason.

To find out the truth of the matter, we must reserve judgement until all the facts are available. What one THINKS about the matter is NOT a fact, it is mere opinion.

Daily life can be approached in a similar way. We can just be a witness to the events going on around us. With this understanding we reserve judgement when judgement is not necessary. We refrain from adding clutter to our mind with opinions. A much more peaceful attitude will then prevail in our life experience.

There will always be so-called POSITIVE and NEGATIVE things/thoughts presenting themselves to our awareness. We need not address everything confronting us from only a positive attitude. A positive attitude, may seem to be productive at first. But without a solid foundation for such an attitude trouble or annoyances seem to have little trouble in making their uninvited appearance. As if by magic they just seem to appear out of nowhere.

Why is that so? That's something else to look into. There is a reason.

Anyhow, these mounting 'negative things' that we keep trying to overcome by a positive attitude just build up more and more tension in us. How long can we cope with that sort of onslaught? Why isn't my positive attitude working?

Well maybe your demand that things should work as you want them to work, is part of the struggle that you are encountering.

We unconsciously *judge* these negative attitudes to be wrong or unpleasant or as "*this shouldn't be*" and so on.

> <u>An attitude of equanimity</u>, frees one from the entanglement of the opposites.

As mentioned earlier, we perceive Life in a dualistic manner. Good-bad, tall-short, peaceful-angry, and so on. Can we just *witness* the way we perceive life and not react on conditioned impulse?

When the time for action comes, you will know it. With an attitude of equanimity, you will not REact to the situation. Instead you will ACT from a place of *clear seeing*. You will intuit the kind of response the situation requires at that moment. It will be the natural thing to do. You will trust it (trust=faith).

This is a much wiser approach to meeting Life's challenges than simply having a positive attitude. Equanimity is superior to assumptions such as positive thinking or a positive attitude.

The enlightened teacher Ramesh Balsekar explained it in this way:

> ---
> *There are two kinds of mind*
> *manifesting in our life experience.*
> *The "thinking mind"*
> *and the "working mind".*
> ---

The "working mind" is the one that does not get INVOLVED in all the "dramas" of life experience that bring suffering (mainly on the psychological level). The "working mind" is the mind that attends to the business of survival, and truly meaningful accomplishments.

The "thinking mind" on the other hand, is the source of all of humanity's problems. The thinking mind is a reactive mind, a mind that takes offence, a mind that can feel insulted or unloved, a mind that constantly seeks perfection but invites more suffering by doing so. The thinking mind is what is known as the personal mind, the possessive mind and so on, and so on, and so on.

Creativity can be sourced through the working mind but never through the thinking mind which has a reactive character. The world of cause and effect is the occupation of the thinking mind.

Take this as you will.

~.~

June (xiv)

The questioner asks: "How would you propose that we get into the habit of living most of our life with the "attitude of equanimity...???"

In the above discourse on positive attitudes, check the paragraphs before the underlined phrase "<u>An attitude of equanimity</u>"

By taking the position of a detached "***witness***" of the events and circumstances that surround us, we can more easily avoid INVOLVEMENT in the dramas that our minds love to engage in.

Being a detached "*witness*" assumes there is no judgement at all of what one is witnessing.

Judgement is the activity of the "thinking" mind. "Witnessing" would be an activity of the "working" mind.

Mind (capital "M"ind as opposed to mind) or <u>working mind</u>, is totally impersonal. There is no Frank, or Mary, or John, or Ray watching or "witnessing" something.

There is ONLY "witnessing" going on. That is total freedom and peace.

The minute the "<u>thinking" mind</u> wants "in on the action" then Frank, or Mary, or John, or Ray are back ... and there is the possibility of trouble brewing.

The "<u>thinking" mind</u> takes everything very personally.

If one sees this happening - then that is the time to take a deep breath.

During such a deep breath, one gains the advantage of a moment of calm.

That moment of calmness provides the <u>"working" mind</u> an opportunity to step into action as the impersonal witness before the "thinking mind gets in on the act".

From the impersonal vantage point of the "working mind" there is no interference of perception by opinion or pre-judgement of any sort.

Not only does one '*see*' clearly what is actually happening around oneself, but also there is the capability to see what is happening **within oneself**.

These are the very first steps to an enlightened view of our life experience.

Anything we say in words is conceptual (thoughts) and not actual.

I have used the words "*thinking*" mind and "*working*" mind as metaphors to talk about how we interact in the world of our experience. I borrowed these terms from Ramesh Balsekar, as I explained in the previous post.

However, this can be discussed in many other ways, using different words, which would still be concepts. (My personal preference is to call the "working" mind "**Mind**" with a capital "M", or impersonal Mind, or Holy Spirit. To what Ramesh calls the "thinking" mind I often give the name "personal mind" or just mind).

Remember, all of these words are just pointers to something beyond what the mind can adequately explain. These words can also to be understood as metaphors that suggest meanings that are subtler than the mind can appreciate.

Even the parables of Jesus were metaphors or stories to illustrate a teaching.

Metaphors and stories/parables are usually easier for people to grasp.

People quickly relate to stories. You are put into the middle of a situation or drama without feeling personally accountable. From such a position you do not feel personally attacked and you may 'learn' something very valuable about yourself. It is sometimes the best doorway to the 'truth'.

Complex conceptual terminology only 'digs a deeper' hole for the "thinking" mind to fall into

The personal mind loves words, ideas, concepts. It creates a personal world with personal stories of a personal life.

> The mind does all of this
> with ease. It has learned
> to do so after generations
> of conditioning.
>
> The mind believes
> that it knows something
> but it fails to understand that
> what it *thinks* it knows is
> only a bunch of words
> ideas, ... thoughts.

Did you ever stop to notice that the words that come out of one's mouth are just **sounds** sounds made by passing breath under pressure from the lungs, through the throat, over the tongue, across the teeth, - then, as this breath escapes the mouth, it is shaped somewhat by quivering lips.

And that production of sound is what the mind has such great faith in. Thoughts being turned into sound. The limitation of thought is made very obvious by this metalphor.

> The limited, finite mind
> cannot possibly
> comprehend
> the Infinite.

The ineffable will always mystify the mental.

Let that be all for now

~.~

June (xv)

I heard it said that someone is thinking in a very "Eastern Way" or a particular ethnic way and so on.

> This is how we characterize thinking in a superficial sense.

> In this way we use such characterizations for identification and for comparison.

"Eastern" and "Western" are characterizations.
These are references that describe thinking as being of some specific character.

> > Thinking is thinking!
> > No matter from what part of the universe.

Thinking
in every case
is characterized
=by an outstanding quality=

That quality is
that thinking
is ALWAYS
*** L I M I T E D ***

~.~

June (xvi)

WHAT ABOUT CHOICES?

Whatever you believe is in the domain of your experience. I would not presume to change your belief in the ability to choose.

The "thinking" mind believes it does or can do many things.

Of a fact, the "thinking" mind called walt, or Ray, or Martha, can think all it wants to think, but it can never regulate the body's physiological system or move the earth or even digest the food that one eats.

The "working" mind (impersonal Mind) is another story. For the impersonal Mind there is no walt, or Ray, or any personality at all. There is only *being*.

Burt Harding summarized it this way - which I like a lot...

We call ourselves HUMAN BEINGS. What does that mean?
In essence, we are BEING playing the HUMAN role.

Scientist/Jesuit priest Pierre Teilhard de Chardin, author of books including "The Phenomenon of Man" and "Le Milieu Divin", put it something like this: (I paraphrase)

We think that we are mere humans seeking to reach the divine,
when in essence we are divinity expressing as human beings.

BEING is totally impersonal and beyond mental comprehension.

The HUMAN is very personal (has personality) and is completely limited in every area of life.

The HUMAN/body/mind mechanism is run by what we might call innate intelligence. The script has been written ... destiny ... DNA ... conditioning determines all.

Then what is choice in that context?

Within that context whatever is perceived as choice becomes part of the harmony or synergy of the destiny.

From a very simple point of view there APPEARS to be choice, and thus one experiences situations where choices are made.

But, consider this. Billions of people over millennia appear to have made choices of all sorts. They made choices to better their "life situation", and yet, time after time what they chose to do did not happen as planned. These "choosers" complete their destiny flawlessly with a synergy that is harmonious with creation.

There are different situations where it "appears" that choosing is involved but in actual fact what is done is a product of "*choiceless* awareness". That is too wide a subject to discuss completely and fairly in the span of a few comments.

A very simplified summary of this topic may be something like this:

The HUMAN role is exemplified by the "*thinking*" mind, the personal mind.

The essence of BEING is most evident in the "*working*" mind, the impersonal mind or the movement of the *Holy Spirit*. (Remember, these are only words, or metaphors. They are pointing beyond the limitations of thought).

Questions such as CHOICE do not exist with the "*working*" mind. What has to be done, is done, because that is the way of choiceless awareness.

The "*thinking*" mind imagines all sorts of things about the actuality of what is. However, whatever it thinks is still just a thought and nothing more.

~.~

July (i)

TIME is a MENTAL Construct.

One can get "lost in time" so to speak.

A pleasurable experience may sometimes seem to pass very quickly– even a whole day (24 hrs) may appear to have taken less time than that.

However an unpleasant situation may seem to last extremely long

Einstein demonstrated that measurements change with changes in acceleration.
MEASURING DEVICES such as rulers get shorter, clocks slow down etc.

> Measurement is a convention
> we have developed.
> Thus we measure
> the passage of events
> by devices such as clocks,
> and call it time.

> We also measure
> passage of events in other ways.
> There is a "psychological clock".
> We experience events.
> These events leave a significant
> psychic impression in the mind,
> such as the birth or death of someone,
> the memory of a particularly pleasant "high"
> (which we then seek to repeat in some way)
> and so on.

A questioner's suggestion of "*successive instants of now...*" actually uses a circular type of argument. .... You make a premise that 'now' is an instant of **time** and then proceed to define that premise as **time**. In essence you are defining **time** as **time**.

> What is an instant?
> An instant or a moment in time
> could last 100 years
> or an entire paleontological era.
> 'Now' in essence is not
> a measure of any dimension.
> It may be considered like
> a 'zero' reference point.
> 'Now' can be
> the current world situation
> as in
> "The state of the world now".

In a universal sense you are NOW, I am NOW - "the NOW generation", etc...

The simplest understanding of TIME is that it is a measurement of some sort of sequence of events, or intervals or groupings of happenings that one wishes to compare. In that sense time is a 'thing' and the 'thing' that time *is*, is a measurement. Are the events taking place within the span of measurement *more* or *less* important than the measurement of the span/interval (time)?

Relatively speaking one could say that both have a certain "relative" importance. Thought can present all sorts of arguments for, or against the proposition. That is what debates are all about. It is a game of power, invented by thought to display the eminence of thought.

The concept of measurement was developed for the purposes of comparison. It is the mind/brain that finds it needs to compare and measure for various reasons. Usually to confirm that it is not being threatened in some way. It is part of the long-time conditioning of the survival instinct.

The most useful comparisons are scientifically based or engineering related. In science we use measurement to compare new results to previous results or to measure the significance of a result against some standard. In engineering related functions, measurement is used to build structures that will be safe compared to unsafe constructions and so on.

So we can see that measurement is a tool of comparison for specific purposes. In the same way that time is a measurement used to compare intervals and sequences which includes such things as speed and acceleration and duration. Again, these are all areas of relative comparisons. No absolutes are possible in the domain of measurement.

> There is no such thing
> as absolute time.
> There is only time
> as a relative measurement
> compared to something else.

Einstein extended the concept to include space using the term SPACE-TIME. But that is a whole other "ball of wax".

Now psychologically speaking, people are very attached to this idea of time. There are emotional attachments to events such as births, and deaths and special occasions.

Thus psychologically, the measure of time is construed in the light of accompanying emotional 'baggage', and so it takes on a 'special' personal meaning. It is in that sense, of personal meaning, that time becomes a 'thing' of the emotional mind.

Many people seem to favour an understanding of time in relationship to their emotional view of reality.

> One final point:
> You cannot experience time itself.
> Nor can you experience
> any measurement unit in itself.
> You cannot experience an inch or a yard.
> What you do experience is the activity of making the measurement or the event or the thing that is being measured.

> > So now where is time?
> > On my watch
> > or some other chronometer
> > I suppose.

It is quite interesting how mankind and its science has done everything to make the concept of time as much of a reality as possible.

It has gotten to the point where many people believe that TIME is a real thing.

It would be some 'feather-in-the-cap' for a sharp investigator to track down and find this thing we call time. You can never capture it and put it behind bars, for it will keep appearing everywhere, no matter what you think you have done to it.

We use the concept of time to measure the passage of events just like we use the concept of an inch, a foot, or a mile (cm, meter and kilometre per international standards) to measure distance.

The symbols that we use to record measurements, such as distance, time, age or volume, are merely conventions. They are conventions for arriving at standard concepts.

Concepts help people to understand one another. People need specific, common reference points for practical purposes such as, "What <u>time</u> shall we meet?", "<u>When</u> will the house be completed?", "What are the <u>dimensions</u> of the living room?", "How <u>far</u> to Borneo?" and so on.

Time makes a good topic for science fiction also. A title such as "When Time Stood Still" is fascinating. Time becomes <u>something</u> to the mind.

    Can you describe time?
    How do I find it?

    Do you have the time?

~.~

July (ii)

Re: Articles espousing "Secrets" of success that made a particular Person "Great" or "Successful"

How does copying an original make you an original?

There must be a lot more to it than just following other people's opinions.

Those who usually follow and try to emulate the "Secrets" of someone's success are often "WANNABEs" (those who Want to Be something) that end up just being duplicate robots or puppets, and do not become as effective as the original.

It may be interesting reading about how someone achieved something.

Do you think you could become like them?

Sure you could, but then you deny your own creative abilities.

You become a "Copy Cat". Some people are good at that. And they make a living entertaining people with their "impressions" of others.

However, if you look carefully, a good impressionist not only learns to copy or emulate the movements and idiosyncrasies of well known people, but a good impressionist also adds the creative touch of putting his "spirit" of life-like illusion into his or her impressionism.

This is the mark of an artist. Not to copy the original, but to see the qualities of the original within oneself and then communicate that originality in a way that is familiar to others.

The true originality, the root of all being, is the same source for all expressions of life, for all humans. It is only from that source that we can create. That is why it is commonly recognizable and admired when a true 'artist' displays their creativity.

You can use any person that inspires you as a **'pointer'** of significance.

But be careful about going overboard (worshiping, etc.). Pointers and guidelines are useful tools – but not for the purpose of copying

Why is it better to user other's "secrets of success" as pointers rather than just copying them?

By copying you miss the experience of learning and understanding directly what it is to be "successful", or what it is, just to have a successful experience.

What is this "success" in relation to who you are and what you do in the world?

Without the direct experiencing of anything, your mind projects an illusory 'world' which you only _think_ that you experience.

Have you seen the movie "The **MATRIX**"? It is like that – an illusion. And you will never know the difference unless there occurs some major challenge to your belief system that you cannot avoid facing.

Why would you want to achieve something that in society's eyes is valuable but in essence means nothing? You ARE society!

It is **people** like you and me who make up society.

It is people like **you** and me who determine what society is and what it can become.

By repeating old value's and old patterns you have nothing new to add, and therefore anything you might call an achievement by society's standards does not really add to your personal growth or spiritual maturation.

Are you at all serious about what or who you are? Do you grasp the significance of your relationship to life.?

~.~

July (iii)

Why do we think what we think?

Is it not possible to witness one's own behaviour in what one says and thinks? What would happen to your so-called life IF:
> compassion and understanding determined what you saw and what you said?

What if you behaved more constructively rather than destructively or lackadaisically in your daily interactions with the world and even in relationship to *your thoughts*? Can you see how discriminating attention would change *your world*?

There is nothing wrong with stating opinions as long as there is no hint of personal attack upon another person. Another's opinion may sometimes motivate change in one's own opinions on a matter.

When one is of fixed opinion on any subject - personal growth and spiritual development are both inhibited.

~.~

July (iv)

Everyone has opinions and preferences that manifest in their lives

These opinions or preferences sometimes appear to provide a 'positive' posture on things.

Anything that we encounter or read will be interpreted through the filter of our personal programming and conditioning.

This includes how we were brought up, our cultural background and influences, and even likes & dislikes that we have added to the character of our persona.

This, all put together, adds to what has been called 'self-image'.

In other words, our programming and conditioning creates the self image of who we **THINK** we are.

But it is not who we actually are. As a hint, recall the movie "The MATRIX".

There is much more depth to you than what you might **think** you are.

One of the perpetual 'battles' that the intellect/ego encounters, is to constantly put us into a position of defending our self-image.

Thought conditions you to believe that your self image is your basic character. The intellect/ego bases its identity on the reflection of self-image.

> I am a doctor: I am an engineer-
> I am overweight: I can't (*whatever*)-
>
> I'm a nice person: I'm a bad person-
> I can never get it right-
> Why am I so stupid-
> —or- I am very smart-
>
> I am a Catholic, or a Protestant, or a Hindu, or whatever.

We literally design our "fake" identities and then live them as if they were real.

It's living a lie. And then we wonder why there are problems in *our life*.

The foregoing is just a minute sampling of what "self-image" implies. Self-image can lead one to believe in such things as their own saintliness or a feeling of total rejection from society. It can lead to feigned "good deeds" as well as to all sorts of villainy and malfeasance.

Sometimes living by one's self-image appears to be working just great. Everything is working out well. *"Everyone likes me, my plans are working out, I have a great future ahead of me,"* and so on. And then one day, totally unexpectedly, a small conflict, or irritation sneaks into that *picture* of a *wonderful life*. Have you seen that old Jimmy Stewart movie *"It's a Wonderful Life"*?

Nothing lasts forever – as they say. Whenever thought claims dominance in making you believe in a self-image then watch out! Sooner or later the *"other shoe will drop"*. It is inevitable where the limitations of thought are given *"carte blanche"* (full powers).

Self-image is also the source of problems of self-confidence and indecisiveness. An in depth study of self is actually the real beginning of the field of Personal Development.

~.~

July (v)

A questioner asks: *How about a rejection from a man ...?*

You use the word "rejection".

That word is creating an image in your mind of what you **think** happened in your limited view in your terms of understanding

You are basing your understanding of his actions from your current emotional outlook on your life situation.

> Do not rush into labelling what happened.
> Do not think that your problem is *sooo* serious.
> Approach it in a detached manner, without self
> investment.
> See this situation as an impartial witness would see it.
> See the situation for what it actually was
> and how it is now affecting your state of mind.

By removing yourself from a state of "personal" involvement there will be more clarity.

> Remove yourself from the introspection.
> Enter a state of just *witnessing*.

> There is no "*you*" witnessing.
> There is just a state of witnessing.
> Non-judgmental, non-reactive
> witnessing, seeing, is happening.
> No "*you*" acting as judge.
> Just observing, and discerning
> what really ***is*** the situation.
> Can you approach you concern in this way?

If you can, then the emotion-filled "you" or "me" will not be there to 'stress out'. You will discern the actual content of what really happened.

It may come to your awareness that the man preferred not to engage in a relationship with someone named "you".

That basically may be the whole story of what happened – without the 'frills' added.

Society has labelled various happenings "rejection" - but it is in error that we do this. The term 'rejection', when applied to oneself personally, can only stir up emotional reactions if you believe in the power of that word.

If you have your self 'vested' in a particular happening, and it does not turn out 'in your favour' - then by your very conditioning the mind will react and create emotional upset in your entire system.

This is the perfect setting for the entrance of "self-image" and the havoc that it can introduce into your life experience.

> *Self-image* proclaims its hurt! *Me – poor me* – why always *me*? – It's his *fault*! – I don't *deserve* this! ...

and more *stress*, and *unhappiness*, and *despondancy* enter your life experience.

Your *self-image*, **"*you*"** personally, feel an attack on your worth as a person.

But, is any of this really true?

Who you really are has not been touched at all!

If you permit yourself to be part of that "story" of hurt, then it will affect you. It will affect you because your self-image is part of every story in your life experiences.

If you believe in the story then you will experience the "reality" of hurt and rejection. You will believe it because you believe in the self-image and the story that it invites

"<u>*Know Thyself*</u>" – This is the beginning of self knowledge. You must learn what "self-image" is all about, and that you are NOT your self-image. It is a role you play in your life story, that is all.

~.~

July (vi)

FEAR & ANXIETY

When I look at fear and anxiety very carefully, I can see that there are phenomena manifesting in two different areas of our experience.

First of all there is physiological 'fear'.

This is the 'fight or flight' mechanism of survival - as it has been called.

When this kind of fear happens, it is a total neurological response.

In such cases thinking does not enter any part of this response.

There is no time to think in a desperate survival situation.

Thinking could delay the instantaneous physiological response that may be necessary for survival. I would not consider this as 'fear' because the word 'fear' does not exist in those situations. There is no thinking about survival, there is only the need for survival and immediate action. There is no time to "*stress out*" over what you should or shouldn't do.

The second aspect of fear is when thought 'kicks-in' or is engaged.

This happens about a moment or two after the reflex survival event.

Thought, intellect/ego, is the "great analyzer" of "*analysis/paralysis*" fame.

This is the purely psychological element of fear - out of which ensues anxiety.

It is the projecting of past events into the "hypothesized" future, a future that in actuality does not exist.

Anxiety is born out of the anticipation that something might happen that we do not know about – in a hypothesized, a supposed, or a dreamed-up future.

Anxiety is about thinking related to "self-image"/ego and its unpredictable future.

From this perspective it could be understood that any conceptualizing (thinking) about the future is a projection of fear. Any possible future event is simply a psychological phenomenon. It is a story created in the mind by thought. The results of such fear projection are unproductive and simply increase anxiety. This increase in anxiety has a stressful effect on the human body.

Please NOTE: We are not here talking about PRACTICAL thinking and planning for future events, meetings, trips etc., which is done by the "working mind"or creative mind, as opposed to the "thinking mind" or ego-centric mind.

In this concept both mind types contain thinking, but each mind type is of a different nature.

The "working mind" thinks in the vertical direction (practical, related to necessities of the moment).

The "thinking mind" thinks in a horizontal direction (projects ideas into a non-existent future, becomes anxious of possible outcomes, and guards "self-image"/ego at all costs.

I wish to clarify, in the context of this dialogue, **thinking about a future:** "Faith in the future" differs somewhat from <u>thinking about the future</u>.

Thinking about the future is ideation and projection into non-existent scenarios and circumstances. It could also be a form of entertainment by thought.

Thought appears to be "playing out" its own stories on a screen of thought energy (the mind).

Faith as I understand it is a completely different matter.

Faith derives from the Latin root "fidere" which means "to trust".

Over the years, the meanings of belief have been added to the word faith and this tends to confuse the understanding of the word 'faith'. Also, in the context of this current dialogue I prefer to avoid any Theological sense of that word 'faith' although it has been used quite properly in some religious contexts.

Faith, taken from its root meaning, is pointing at a sense of trust and unshakable confidence that defies any thinking about it all.

This is almost the way that Paul uses it in Hebrews 11:1 –

"Now faith is the substance of things hoped for, the evidence of things not seen."

The above quote relates a strong sense of confidence and trust that surpasses thought. It is only when you make up reasons (or excuses) for such trust (faith) that the thinking process is engaged. Then you need words to explain somehow what you mean.

An action of faith or confidence can be carried out with no thinking at all

Let's clarify that statement: There will be no thought involved in the actual matter of faith or confidence, but thinking can still exist concurrently.

If your attention goes to the thinking that is contrary to the faith that you start out with and you start to "believe" in the thoughts, then you give power to the thoughts and they will trump the faith.

So 'faith' is like confidence and trust (like in confidential meaning a matter of trust). You might arrive at the faith through a thinking process. That usually results after correct discernment of what one is observing and thinking. But as soon as a state of faith has been established, and you remain focused on that faith to the exclusion of opposing thoughts then that trust, that confidence becomes your "guiding light".

And it doesn't take much faith:

"... if you had faith as a grain of mustard seed, ..."
(Matthew 17:20 and Luke 17:6)

~.~

<u>July (vii)</u>

Just a reminder that you are NOT your body, or anything physical or mental.

Those are just extensions or appearances of what you really are.

They are the vehicles through which you express in this world.

If you are looking for somebody (i.e. another 'body' - a physical thing) to complete or to fulfil you then this may <u>seem</u> to fulfil your needs for a while, but it is not a real solution – it is only the phantom of a solution (as you probably already know).

Looking for just a 'body' to be your partner brings in the factor of comparison, and then you are looking at your body also, and the factor of "self-image" becomes colossal!

So the question you will ultimately put to yourself is – "What am I really looking for?"

"If what I have been looking for has brought disappointment and pain, then do I really understand what relationship really means?"

If your existing ideas of relationship, and the ideas given to you by other people regarding relationship have not worked for you, then perhaps you are ready or a deeper understanding of what your life experience is all about?

=*=

You are so much more
than what
you THINK you are.

=*=

July (viii)

Everybody! must have done something right to be where they are today.

Think about that for a moment:
- if you are successful
  you must have done something right to be successful.
- if you are a mess
  you must have done something right to be a mess.

Or possibly, you have nothing to do with any of this.

Do we believe in a particular reality based only on "circumstantial evidence"? Could that be clouding our understanding?

What about discernment? How can that help clarify understanding of our life experiences?

I will meditate upon that.

– Will you join me?

~.~

July (ix)

Many articles and guidelines have been written on how to organize oneself to "save" time and to make most of the available time, and so on.

Many of these are quite practical and useful guidelines in the "work world".

However, experience has brought to my attention that the actual secret is to make use of such guidelines to your advantage, but **NOT IN THE CONTEXT OF TIME**.

Do you believe that a mental construct like time has some sort of power or influence over the brain's innate mechanism for seeking order?

Wouldn't such a belief add a psychological obstacle (possibly unconsciously)?

If you believe in time, then might you not get anxious about some future event? This adds a stress load to the whole body system.

That is the psychological obstacle that I was talking about in the second question above.

To be organized with various aids, and methods is to be prudent in practical affairs.

To give credence to something called time as if it had some sort of 'power' or role to play or not to play in the execution of a productive personal economy, is hardly efficacious (*effective*).

~.~

July (x)

If personal development is viewed from an intellectual level only, then the results will be limited and not long lasting.

It is at the level of the "heart" (not the organ but one might say the spiritual level of connection) that one realizes the meanings of one's experiences in life and true relationship to life.

This is NOT a topic that most people with only an interest in "Ordinary" PD (Personal Development) can comprehend. Ordinary PD takes place at the intellect/ego level.

It is the training of the "puppet", the personality, that thing that most people THINK or believe they *are*. And that level of understanding, is of course, limited to the world of psychological dramas, which are witnessed in various conflicting interactions.

Next time you are involved in a "personality drama" just **watch the thoughts** and see if you can witness the handiwork of thought in action.

~.~

July (xi)

Here is an opinion expressed by many people:
"I believe that more money can increase happiness by reducing stress ..." or some other reason.

This sort of reasoning does not explain why some people who are at very low income levels are quite happy. And in many cases they seem to experience much less stress than those with significantly more disposable income.

Thus, although money may appear to be helpful, and can be, in some cases, it is definitely not the answer to touching the source of happiness.

Money and material things... Well money *is* a material thing.

And thoughts also, are material things!

Material things may bring temporary happiness for a week, a month, a year, ten years or whatever.

But the "flavour" of that happiness would have some of that "bitter-sweet" quality to it. It would not be permanent and not free of worry.

There will always be a nagging undercurrent of uncertainty, of insecurity,
– what will happen when the money,
or the things that keep me feeling happy,
are no longer bountifully manifesting
in my life experience?

To rely on some<u>THING</u> or someone, to put you into a state of happiness is misdirected understanding. You are the very source of happiness itself.

Tap that source at the root!

What is the root? (more meditation – I may have already discussed it earlier. Or I will later on).

Tap the source of all happiness at the root of being.(some people use other terminology like - God, or Spirit, or Holy Spirit, or Energy, or Universal Intelligence, or Higher Self or Your True Self or the NOW or the Christ).

These are all words and words are never the thing in itself. Words are mere representations – they point to another reality – the one that is beyond personal mind.

So, definitely! *tap that source – the source of being.*

Then, whether there be money or not, there will be joy.

~.~

July (xii)

A forum participant states: *"Having no problem means that a person is either dead, drunk or insane..."*

I see this attitude regarding problems as a great misconception.

The human mind evolved to deal with problems. Initially it was problems of survival.

Over millions of years the human brain/mind complex became an efficient problem solver – except where it started to project non-existent problems into the future

When the mind started to project into the future, things that had not yet happened, and might never happen, you added another chapter to the dream.

In some cases you may need to plan for the future, but when that future involves projections of egoic identity then trouble is brewing.

This is where anxiety eventually takes hold, and perhaps insanity may follow in some cases. But that is because there is a focus on problems instead of a creative view of seeing opportunities where others see only problems.

At the level of mind, those 'problem-free' opportunities can only be grasped by inspiration, which is not of the intellect/mind.

If the efficient problem solving mechanism sticks to the practicalities of everyday living (i.e. if you use thinking for practical purposes), –
> then all appears to go well.

- ✓ When thinking is based on egoic interests;
- ✓ when personal mind is occupied with problems projected into the future;
- ✓ when unreal, not actual, unmanifested problems occupy daily mind activity;

then the mental ground becomes fertile for all sorts of psychological crises.

Psychological (mental) crises develop because there are a multitude of complex interrelated issues presented, all seemingly demanding your attention. And your attention will go there if you give credence (believe) that what thought is projecting as future probabilities is 'real'. Belief makes it real to the personal thought system.

When the intellect/ego pursues a desired solution to anything then it easily fails to discern the relationship of thinking *about* problems to *actually existing* problems. There is no relationship!

Problems you think about only exist in the mind.

Problems are made of mind stuff – they are made of thoughts.

With a bit of discernment you can see what is just plain ordinary thinking of problems and what is actually a problem facing you RIGHT NOW. It is only what is obviously 'in front of you' that needs your undivided attention.

With discernment intelligence comes into action and then thought is used as a valid tool rather than a projector of attention grabbing drama.

"No problems" is not in the domain of mind. "No problems" is the ability to see beyond the limitations of conditioned thought.

~.~

July (xiii)

Lao Tsu on Success

Here is an ancient eastern view on the subject of Success.

It comes from a very short book of wisdom called "Tao Te Ching" roughly pronounced Dow Deh Jing.

The "Tao Te Ching" was written around the 6th century BCE by the sage Lao Tzu ("Old Master"). The oldest excavated text dates back to the late 4th century BCE.

The comments on success are from Chapter 13 of 81 very short (one-page) chapters.

- <u>Tao Te Ching on Success</u> -

> *Success is as dangerous as failure.*
> *Hope is as hollow as fear.*

What does it mean that success is as dangerous as failure?

> *Whether you go up the ladder or down it,*
> *your position is shaky.*

When you stand with your two feet on the ground, you will always keep your balance.

What does it mean that hope is as hollow as fear?

> *Hope and fear are both phantoms*
> *that arise from thinking of the self.*
> *When we don't see the self as self,*
> *what do we have to fear?*

>> *See the world as your self.*
>> *Have faith in the way things are.*
>> *Love the world as your self;*
>> *then you can care for all things.*

~.~

July (xiv)

THE WISDOM of the TAO (dow)

= In reference to the Tao Te Ching =

To understand this wisdom you have to study the entire 81 chapters and follow through on the inner depth of the philosophy of life associated with it.

> The Tao is the wisdom of the way.
> The major concept is ONENESS.

Everything in all the universes that could possibly exist is united as one whole consciousness or God, or energy, or emptiness, or space, or silence, or being.

In fact, a name cannot even be given to it,
the Tao confirms this in the first few lines of chapter 1:

The Tao that can be told
is not the eternal Tao.
The name that can be named
is not the eternal Name

The unnameable is the eternally real.
Naming is the origin
of all particular things.

Free from desire, you realize the mystery.
Caught in desire, you see only the manifestations.

Therefore, when one jumps to ANY conclusion about any such wisdom, then you know that you don't understand it.

All the great wisdom teachings cannot be truly comprehended intellectually. The deepest understanding of such teachings is sourced intuitively.

There is nothing to learn, nothing to memorize.

There is only that which can be directly experienced.

However, the moment thought/mind/intellect enters the picture –

then one is strictly dealing with the world of manifestation, (the world of Maya, the dream or illusion). Most of Buddhism, Advaita teachings, and some Hinduism, source this wisdom directly.

Christianity often subtly references the teachings first proclaimed in the Tao and other sources.

Jesus' saying "Love your neighbour as yourself" is reminiscent of the Tao's "Love the world as your self". They are both teaching the same wisdom.

The words attributed to Jesus in some cases allude to this ONENESS as the GODHEAD which is different from God the Father etc.

Wikipedia puts it this way:

"Godhead is a Middle English variant of the word godhood, and denotes the Divine Nature or Substance (Ousia) of the Christian God, or the Trinity."

The actual wisdom spoken of in the Tao has nothing to do with human doctrines that have been designed by religions with specifically intended outcomes.

(An side note that may have relevance): Masters like Jesus did not formulate doctrines.

Those who followered and sincerely wished to preserve his teachings developed a religion based on his teachings. These people relied on formalizing what they perceived to be *truths* that *must not be questioned.*

Questioning could lead to something other, or something beyond what they intended to preserve.

Thus we can see how the limitations of thought can establish well-intentioned doctrines and dogmas. But these are as limited as the thought system that produced them.

Words *are* **pointers** *to the truth, but words are incapable of conveying the truth itself.*

In this context where does Personal Development or even spiritual growth fit in?

If we are to love our neighbour or the world as our self - this does not mean "like our self" but actually "as our self".

Under the wisdom of oneness we are all ONE.

What we see as many is only in the realm of manifestation. That which is manifested has its source in the unmanifest – but it all is.interconnected and imbued with *beingness*.

This puts a much deeper understanding on what Personal Development or spiritual maturation could be. If you can really look into it deeply you will be amazed!

~.~

July (xv)

ACHIEVING PERSONAL GOALS

Achievement of personal goals must be viewed in its proper context.

In the practical sense, in the world of employment and survival needs there does appear to be a need to set goals – and even in this area it is not critical since things can be rescheduled, re-planned and changed.

Keeping one's attention in the wrong place can lead to more sorrow, and thus possible moments of joy slip away.

I am much more inclined to cherishing each moment with everything that it brings - be it pain, sorrow, or happiness.

This is living life to the fullest without denial or regret, not judging or even having the thought "Why me?"- when it does not go as you expect it to go.

Setting goals may be one of the most artificial things one can do in life. It is to deny the spontaneous interaction with the sacredness of Life.

I am not talking here of the practical need of scheduling appointments, planning vacations and outings, organizing one's finances, etc.

It is wisdom to take care of practical matters, and it is also wisdom to allow every moment as Life expresses through you as one of its manifestations.

If you want to speak in terms of 'goals' then my response would be that my goals are met each and every moment, and I did not even have to set them.

I understand myself to be a part of the mystery of Life and I share it with joy with anyone who wishes to share.

~.~

July (xvi)

Paradoxes appear to be a strictly intellectual phenomenon.

It is what we perceive and then interpret mentally.

Both sides/alternatives of a paradox
point to truth.

> However, in both cases,
> because it is intellectualized,
> it can only be a relative truth -
> relative to previous knowledge,
> the limitations of understanding,
> conditioning, etc.

The paradox seems to exist because intellectual nowledge is a matter of condensing the perceived experiences in life into a conceptual framework for purposes of easy reference and comparison.

The mind is always comparing and evaluating

> It believes that it has to feel secure
> – that it can take no chances.
> This is a remnant of the survival instinct.

Theoretical processing of information (scientific method etc.) formulates working hypotheses; but when confronted by that which is not measurable or comparable in any logical or physical sense, the intellect insists on the value of its scientific (knowledge) base.

The contradiction stares the logic of scientific investigation in the face defying any measurement or analysis. Nonetheless, the intellect insists on understanding the contradiction in relative terms. It will make a theory to explain it. And that seems to satisfy it for a while.

> This is intellectual paradox.
> The relative is always in a state
> of hypothesis and possible change.
> The absolute is beyond hypothesis
> and yet encompasses all possibilities
> of growth and change.

~.~

July (xvii)

People feel great when they experience what is called success. They refer to it as **personal** success. But it is not really personal success. It is just the completion of some task, or project, or agenda, or other achievement. It is the completion event which releases a lot of pent up stress and/or anxiety and puts one in a relaxed state.

Finally reaching the "end", one gets a feeling of completion and relief. It feels so good just to be unencumbered, no more need to carry all that highly-tensioned thinking in one's mind. You feel relaxed, maybe even elated to some degree that you finally "did it". You feel *successful!* Personally successful.

One can claim ownership and say "I did it", but that is not my bent in life. Any such claim usually leads to "suffering" of some sort when the next project does not culminate in successful completion.

That sort of failure leaves a mark on one's self-image. Then in your mind '*you*' becomes a failure.

So there is wisdom, reason and value in not claiming success or failure as a personal attribute in any sense.

NOBODY IS A SUCCESS OR FAILURE!

You are merely involved in VENTURES OF SUCCESS OR FAILURE.

Things (including human bodies) - come and go, grow, change and die. - What you really are, is not a thing. Thus for you, there can be no failure.

When we start to talk of things like 'financial success', it appears to be a bit more difficult for people to separate self-image from actuality.

There may be *successful* financial transactions or financial losses. If you are a person who identifies with lack and the need to have – if you cannot escape the lure of those dollar signs $$$, then **you** may end up feeling as a success or as a failure. You are then *believing* that you *are* the self-image.

Remind yourself that you are infinitely more than what you *think* you are.

~.~

July (xviii)

> In essence our experience of life is about the journey.
>
> It is not about you and me or them.
> It is only about the journey.
>
> In the context of the journey we encounter all our experiences.
>
> If we get attached to the experiences then we lose the focus of the journey.
>
> The journey includes how we relate to life.
> The journey is EVERYTHING!

~.~

July (xix)

Tao te Ching - Lao Tsu - Chapter 33

----

*Knowing others is intelligence;
knowing yourself is true wisdom.
Mastering others is strength;
mastering yourself is true power.*

*If you realize that you have enough,
you are truly rich.
If you stay in the centre
and embrace death with your whole heart,
you will endure forever.*

~.~

July (xx)

Have you noticed that many articles use the word 'secret' or 'secrets' to grab a reader's attention?

Have you ever thought why that might work?

Many people are seeking that which will make them happy or happier in one way or another.

To be free of daily drudgery and worries is another hope of many. Constantly one compares one's own state of life and feelings to another's.

"Oh, if only I could have what she/he has", — or
"If *x* or *y* happened to me then everything would be just great".

or — "I hope that *doesn't* happen to me".

Comparison is the "Achilles heal" of the personal self.

Secrets ... What an alluring word!
Always someone else seems to have
a secret *that may solve all my problems.*

Not so!

The way out of this "secret" dilemma is to understand that at the root, at the core, at the 'heart' level
ALL PEOPLE ARE THE SAME!

Yes, personalities differ - these are only manifestations of the world in which we experience this particular chapter of life. This all happens at the phenomenal level of life.

If you like the word "secret", then the real secret is within you. This has been told by sages throughout the ages.

Jesus said, "The kingdom of heaven is *within you*"— heaven being that place of happiness and perfection that many seem to constantly strive for.

J. Krishnamurti called it "The kingdom of happiness". Many other words have been used: Nirvana, etc., etc., etc...

No, I am not talking religion or myth.

I am talking experiential fact. That "secret" that many seek is within them.

Learn first to understand the consequences of self-image. Then find out what may lay beyond that limitation of attachment to a self-image.

~.~

July (xxi)

From what might be called the spiritual perspective FEAR is the opposite of LOVE.

Fear implies separation, fragmentation, the unknown "other", unwillingness to face an actuality, etc.

Love implies oneness, wholeness, completeness, understanding, sufficiency and embracing life as that which animates every living thing.

~.~

July (xxii)

Lao Tsu - Tao Te Ching

Chapter 79

Failure is an opportunity.
If you blame someone else,
there is no end to the blame.

Therefore the Master
fulfils his/her own obligations
and corrects her/his own mistakes.
She/He does what she/he needs to do
and demands nothing of others.

~.~

July (xxiii)

The Nature of Opinion

> Watch people in conversation.
> They may be politicians, or bankers.
> Watch sports show hosts in discussion
> or watch them interviewing
> an athlete of any sport.

Have you watched talk show hosts in action?
Or maybe you have seen
a popular psychologist appearing
on a popular talk show.

> How about advertisers – of any ilk?
> They are always playing a game
> of "Ours is the best available…"

Then there are editorial writers.
They have much to say,
and so on…

All of the above use the currency of *opinion* for various reasons. However, it does feel nice, when you express yourself, and let another know that this is *you* saying something important coming from *you*. There is nothing wrong with self expression and it can be an adventure that leads to greater awareness if you give sufficient attention to each moment of such expression. There you may find many *secrets* of human behaviour and innocence that we all share in common.

However, if that self-expression solidifies into *opinion* then it becomes truly limited and has no more scope than the mind from which it arises.

Opinion is centred around a fixed locus.

From any dictionary one can arrive at an understanding of what opinion entails. For example:

Opinion is - A view or judgment formed about something, not necessarily based on fact or knowledge.

   _or_

Opinion is - The *beliefs* or views of a large number or majority of people about a particular thing.

You will, of course, find many variations on the meaning. Would that be because of opinion, or because different interpreters wish the word to be seen in a particular light? Or is that still a kind of opinion? Or is it just a different way of expressing the same thing? — Can you see the difficulty of obtaining precision of clarity with words?

The value of an opinion to the bearer or taker of a particular opinion is always personalized. How an individual values a thought (opinion) is based on conditioning of various sorts. Thus the content of an opinion may be understood to be illusory.

About opinions ...

> ===> **Could it be *thought* having fun?** <===

Can I interest you in "The Game of Opinions?" I asked.

She wondered, "What is that?"

"The Game of Opinions?" I repeated.

"Yes, what ***is*** the Game of Opinions?" she demanded.

"Well, if you *must* know, it can be described as Intellectual Tag," I replied.

"Let's make it into a *slogan*!" she exclaimed.

"And ***how*** might we word it?" I asked

She took out her black magic marker,

pulled out a large piece of white card paper,

and neatly wrote, in large letters:

The Game of Opinions
– an Intellectual Tag.
A forum where thought
– can make its brag.

~.~

July (xxiv)

Is there a difference between self confidence and self esteem or are they one and the same?

Self-confidence relates to how sure you feel about yourself as an effective individual when relating to others

Self-confidence also has to do with how you judge your personal ability, and power. ...Here *power* means your ability and effectiveness in influencing others.

In a non-personal context, <u>confidence</u> is not the same as <u>self-confidence.</u> The characteristics may appear to be the same, but <u>confidence</u> is impersonal whereas <u>self-confidence</u> is focused on the <u>self-image</u>.

Confidence is a trust. You might say trust at a 'gut' level where self-image cannot reach. Self-confidence is tightly focused on the secure feeling of the self-image. It is limited whereas impersonal confidence is beyond conceptual limitations.

Self-esteem is the overall appraisal you personally make of your own worth.

> **Beliefs** are involved in self-esteem.
> Beliefs such as: "I am competent",
> "I am worthy", or its opposite
> "I don't deserve it",
> "I am unworthy", etc.

Limiting beliefs about self worth and competence could also be in between the extremes of being either competent or incompetent, and between worthy and unworthy.

The lack of self-esteem is very evident when negative beliefs, such as, "Nobody cares about me", "I am useless", etc. constantly occupy one's thoughts. This sort of attitude or understanding about oneself often leads to despair.

And, there are also emotions involved in self-esteem — emotions such as triumph, despair, pride and shame.

Self esteem relates in some way to the beliefs one holds onto regarding personal worth.

This is just a brief overview...

~.~

July (xxv)

There are many ideas that have been put forth for acquiring **improved** self-confidence, but if you do not already have an intuitive feeling for how you relate to the rest of society then any such practices as described herein, are likely to lead to only an artificial representation of self-confidence.

Taking it the other way around — if you are self-confident then it is very likely that you may display most of the characteristics outlined in this article, -*or*- maybe none of them.

Who says you have to be a "copy-cat" in anything. It's your life experience. There is something about uniqueness that should not be overlooked.

It may be profitable for an individual to first evaluate why they feel that they need to build self-confidence.

Certainly NOT because someone else says so!

Do some careful introspection of your thoughts/ideas and feelings about the need for self confidence building.

By giving this sort of careful attention to any desire or need you are more likely to touch the truth of any matter.

Introspection is a very direct approach to knowing yourself and it avoids falling into the trap of following the opinions of others.

If the opinions of others appeal to you then some introspection on how those opinions relate to your particular desire or need will be most productive.

Self-confidence is not something "out there", or a matter of "*do steps 1 to 10, —and you will <u>make it</u>*".

Self-confidence has to do with *self*, and who but yourself is closest to dealing with it? You may look at various sources as "pointers" to the solution, and of course that may help you to find the real solution in yourself. Any other approach is bound to be artificial and not long-lasting.

You decide! It's only your personal experiencing that will know for sure.

~.~

<u>July (xxvi)</u>

Chapter 59 (wisdom from **Tao Te Ching**)

> ...
> The mark of a moderate man
> is freedom from his own ideas.
> Tolerant like the sky,
> all-pervading like sunlight,
> firm like a mountain,
> supple like a tree in the wind,
> he has no destination in view
> and makes use of anything
> life happens to bring his way.
>
> Nothing is impossible for him.
> Because he has let go,
> he can care for the people's welfare
> as a mother cares for her child.

~.~

July (xxvii)

In answer to a questioner:

Yes, Maslow does state the basic needs.
How those needs are met is a different area of exploration.

Morality is conceptual, whereas needs are actual - man has to survive to be able to moralize –

– and moralization leads to a whole "other ball of wax".

~.~

July (xxviii)

— *in response to an article posted on the forum entitled:* **Dress for Success** *"Dress for the job you want"*...

Perhaps when it comes to actual hiring it is only important that the person does not look like they don't care for themselves (by how they dress).

Fancy clothes etc., are not the main criteria - although it might prevent one from being 'dismissed' from a job interview.

If you dress like a banker while applying for a position at the butcher's — I wonder?

How do doctors and great surgeons dress? — or applicants for those positions?

This "Mr. Dressup" Business doesn't really 'hold water'.

It may have some limited applications - like
running for president perhaps —
you know - to impress the public, and so on...

Actually I liked watching the "Mr. Dressup"
TV show with my son when he was a child.
The 'dressing up' was related
to what jobs the people actually did.

Well that doesn't really work beyond
the basic level of teaching a child -
—could you just imagine people
dressing up as police men or women
to apply for a position on the police force?

> So much for dress-up theory!
> As long as it looks like you have given
> some care to dressing for
> a particular occasion,
> without going bankrupt
> or missing a bill payment,
> then you pass the course on
> 'Dress Up'.
>
> Dressing up may be a by-product
> of the phenomenon of success
> but not a determinant.
>
> The main success in dressing up
> is getting your close on properly.

~.~

July (xxix)

Ah yes! The simple pleasures of life.

To take a deep breath and slowly let it out,
without a single thought on your mind...

To know 'I exist'
- you can feel it viscerally
and no amount of theorizing
or opinion can change
the simple pleasure and reality
that "I exist"!

The simple pleasures...
They don't have to be proven,
They don't have to be defended,
They don't have to be explained.
They just ***are***.

Simple pleasures are what you *are*
in essence, in the moment –

Thought
for one instant,
recedes,
and the experience
is presence.

~.~

July (xxx)

Basically, we are all actors on the stage of life.
We assume roles which vary with circumstance and people.

As parents, we play 'Mother/Father' character roles.
As employers we play the 'boss' character role.
Among people we would like to impress, we play the 'so happy to meet you' role and other variations.
Among people we wish to avoid,
there are other roles that we assume
depending on the impression we wish to leave.

Similarly - "Charming one" is a role
to display *class*, or importance, or whatever.
It can be a fun game if you do not take it seriously.

So, when do we play **ourselves**?
This question is in reference to integrity
— which means wholeness, completeness.

If we cannot be comfortable with being ourselves
then we will wear many
different masks to hide behind.
By avoiding the reality of self
we miss the opportunity to actually *grow*
in conscious understanding
of what is really going on in our life experience.

There is more joy in discovering who we really *are*
and then playing all the roles you want,
because then those roles will have a depth,
a flavour of 'je ne sais quoi'

perhaps something mysteriously
attractive or touching.

~.~

July (xxxi)

"...the whole world belongs to you."

To seriously pursue such a dialogue one of the first requirements would be that you would have to put aside (not permanently-just for the dialogue)
any beliefs you held about anything that might interfere with the investigation that we would pursue.

It is like a criminal investigation
or a trial in a court of law.

If you BELIEVE someone to be guilty before you truly investigate the facts,
then you may convict the wrong person.
(just an example)

First—all personal beliefs must be set aside
Next—begin an unbiased investigation into the matter

Otherwise you live based on beliefs and not actuality.
Of course you can still have some beliefs
about various things,
but deep down
you realize that they are just 'modes'
or ways of looking at things.

The actuality is part of the inner being and has nothing to do with personality, or intellect/thought (which includes beliefs).

Belief is simply a way of thinking.

When you repeatedly, habitually think the same way about something over an extended period, you become conditioned to that way of thinking. That way of thinking becomes comfortable and feels a part of you. You may get so comfortable with the way you think that it becomes easy and almost demanding to defend the position held by thought.

This may even entail great personal cost or sacrifice. And this is all done just to defend a thought, a concept or an idea. To defend that which is temporal.

This is the danger of belief without discernment.

People once believed the earth was flat.

Belief is a useful tool.

We use belief to take place of *that* which we really
do not know about,
or are not certain of,

To find out – we investigate in various ways,

Soon we uncover (discover) the actuality—
for example: the earth is spherical and—
it orbits the sun.

When we discover the truth of the matter,
we can discard the previously held belief
because now the actuality presents itself
to our awareness.

This is just a small example of what I mean by discovering through serious investigation, and discernment. And this can be done either by personal introspection or in dialogue with another similarly inclined person.

~.~

July (xxxii)

Tao Te Ching ... Chapter 44

Fame or integrity: which is more important?
Money or happiness: which is more valuable?
Success or failure: which is more destructive?

If you look to others for fulfilment,
you will never truly be fulfilled.
If your happiness depends on money,
you will never be happy with yourself.

Be content with what you have;
rejoice in the way things are.
When you realize there is nothing lacking,
the whole world belongs to you.

~.~

July (xxxiii)

A response to a forum member's personal concern...

You express that you have a certain type of 'fear' of "leaving the door open" for abuse. Personally, I do not believe that is actually possible. Any verbal abuse felt by an individual on this or any forum, or even in person, would be how they personally viewed their own vulnerability.

I understand that there is such a thing as abusive language and so on, and it is, generally speaking, a display of what one might call "uncultured behaviour", in a supposedly culturally civilized society. But that alone is just so many words and thoughts.

Words and thoughts have no power whatsoever over another individual, unless, of course, you feel threatened by such words and thoughts. Then one would have to find out if the threat is real or not. Is there a hidden psychological insecurity (usually self-image related), or is there evidence of impending physical threat?

Compassion and understanding are useful attitudes to embody in one's behaviour and relations with others.

~.~

And so it ends...

For NOW...

----- Watching thought can be liberating. -----

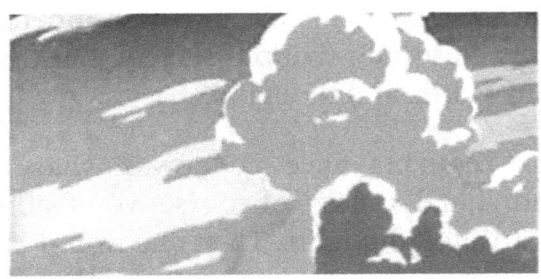

www.ingramcontent.com/pod-product-compliance
Lightning Source LLC
Chambersburg PA
CBHW060321050426
42449CB00011B/2592